Fighting the Plague in Antiquity and the Middle Ages: The History of Ancient and Medieval Efforts to Prevent the Spread of Diseases

By Charles River Editors

Josse Lieferinxe's painting of St. Sebastian pleading with Jesus for the life of a gravedigger affected by the Plague of Justinian

About Charles River Editors

Charles River Editors provides superior editing and original writing services across the digital publishing industry, with the expertise to create digital content for publishers across a vast range of subject matter. In addition to providing original digital content for third party publishers, we also republish civilization's greatest literary works, bringing them to new generations of readers via ebooks.

Introduction

A medieval depiction of plague victims being buried

Plague and pestilence have both fascinated and terrified humanity from the very beginning. Societies and individuals have struggled to make sense of them, and more importantly they've often struggled to avoid them. Before the scientific age, people had no knowledge of the microbiological agents – unseen bacteria and viruses – which afflicted them, and thus the maladies were often ascribed to wrathful supernatural forces. Even when advances in knowledge posited natural causes for epidemics and pandemics, medicine struggled to deal with them, and for hundreds of years religion continued to work hand-in-hand with medicine.

Inevitably, that meant physicians tried a variety of practices to cure the sick, and many of them seem quite odd by modern standards. By the time Rome was on the rise, physicians understood that contagions arose and spread, but according to Galen, Hippocrates, and other Greco-Roman authorities, pestilence was caused by *miasma*, foul air produced by the decomposition of organic matter. Though modern scientists have since been able to disprove this, on the face of it there was some logic to the idea. Physicians and philosophers (they were very often the same, Galen being an example) noticed that disease arose in areas of poor sanitation, where filth and rotting matter was prevalent and not disposed of, and the basic measures to prevent disease – waste removal, provision of clean food and water and quarantining - would have been obvious to them. The scenting of miasmic air with incense and other unguents to expel the foulness would also have thus made sense, though people now know that can't stop the spread of a disease.

Ancient physicians at the time believed that *miasma* was not the direct cause of disease but rather a catalyst. Maladies were caused by an imbalance of what Galen called the four humors. According to him (and Hippocrates before him), the body contained four kinds of fluids: black bile, yellow bile, blood, and phlegm. These corresponded to the four elements of which the entire universe was composed: earth, fire, water, and air. Black bile was tied to earth, yellow bile to fire, blood to air, and phlegm to water. It was believed that the balance of the humors in the body not only determined an individual's health, but their behavior and temperament as well. A melancholic (from *melanos*, the word for "black") disposition was caused by an excess of black bile. Yellow bile made a person fiery or choleric (from *khole*, the word for bile), while a phlegmatic (from *phlegma*, body moisture) temperament denoted a surplus of phlegm. The most desirable temperament was the sanguine (*sanguis*, blood), which exhibited happiness, calm and enthusiasm. The ancient Romans thought *miasma* caused an imbalance in these fluids, and disease resulted. For the ancient physician, as indeed for all physicians for the next 1,500 years or so, illness was not the direct result of external agents.

The theory of the four humors was based on philosophy rather than what today would be called science. It might seem easy to ridicule the idea in hindsight, but the ancient philosophers and doctors did not and could not possess the elementary scientific knowledge that medical practitioners have today, so humorism can be seen as an honest attempt to make sense of the human body and its malignancies.

The High Middle Ages had seen a rise in Western Europe's population in previous centuries, but these gains were almost entirely erased as the plague spread rapidly across all of Europe from 1346-1353. With a medieval understanding of medicine, diagnosis, and illness, nobody understood what caused Black Death or how to truly treat it. As a result, many religious people assumed it was divine retribution, while superstitious and suspicious citizens saw a nefarious human plot involved and persecuted certain minority groups among them.

Though it is now widely believed that rats and fleas spread the disease by carrying the bubonic plague westward along well-established trade routes, and there are now vaccines to prevent the spread of the plague, the Black Death gruesomely killed upwards of 100 million people, with helpless chroniclers graphically describing the various stages of the disease. It took Europe decades for its population to bounce back, and similar plagues would affect various parts of the world for the next several centuries, but advances in medical technology have since allowed researchers to read various medieval accounts of the Black Death in order to understand the various strains of the disease.

It was only in the mid-19th century that scientists established a definitive link between viruses and bacteria and disease, and this allowed the development of vaccines to prevent the spread of killers such as smallpox, typhus, and diphtheria. In the early 20th century, the development of antibiotics helped immensely, but as the Spanish flu of 1918 and the recent Coronavirus has demonstrated, people have not succeeded in conquering all infectious diseases, and the fear of contagion remains with humanity.

Fighting the Plague in Antiquity and the Middle Ages: The History of Ancient and Medieval Efforts to Prevent the Spread of Diseases looks at the ways past societies have striven to cope with epidemics and the various remedies – some bizarre, some desperate, others logical but nonetheless misguided – they employed. The approaches include an eclectic mix of medicine, supernatural rituals, religion, natural philosophy, and the use of scientific advances. Along with pictures depicting important people, places, and events, you will learn about ancient and medieval efforts to fight the plague like never before.

Gods and Demons

The earliest record of any kind of systematized healthcare dates to ancient Mesopotamia and the Sumerian and Babylonian civilizations. For these, healing was in the gift of the gods and physicians operated as their instruments. The goddess Gula ("the great physician") presided over medicine for the ancient Sumerians.[1] Her son Ninazu was also a healer and assisted her. Ninazu was represented holding a rod around which a serpent was wound, and the snake became a recurring symbol of the medical profession that survives to this day.[2] Ninazu was also god of the underworld and so was master both of death and life. Just as the serpent shed its skin and renewed itself, so Ninazu gave deliverance to his supplicants.[3]

For the ancient Egyptians who took up the mantle of Mesopotamian physicians, medicine channelled the power of the gods. It is often noted that ancient Egyptian medicine was advanced for its time and more enlightened in many respects than that of the Middle Ages. Egyptian physicians were aware of the importance of diet; they employed medicines, had a fairly good (though not complete) knowledge of human anatomy, recognized the healing properties of massage and aromatherapy, and performed surgery, including trepanning. A major source of medical knowledge was the practice of embalming and mummification of bodies in preparation for the afterlife, which was performed by priests. Thus, ancient Egyptian priests were also physicians.

The Egyptians understood that the heart was the center of the blood supply, though they believed it also moved tears, urine and semen.[4] Indeed, they held that the heart was the source of all vitality and health and also the seat of emotion and intelligence. The concept has survived symbolically to this day in common parlance, but for the Egyptians the heart was the *jb* that had to be preserved after death to ensure an individual's survival in the afterlife.

In time, Egyptian priests became adept at healing fractures and other injuries, prescribing herbal medicines, performing simple surgery, and even treating mental illnesses.[5] When it came to the treatment of contagion, however, they were at a loss and attributed pestilence to the influence of gods and demons. While it's easy to ridicule that belief today, there was simply no way for the ancients to have known of microbiological organisms as the source of infection. Indeed, the theory that diseases were caused by microorganisms would not be definitively proven until the late 19th century.[6]

---

[1] Joshua J. Mark, "Health Care in Ancient Mesopotamia", *Ancient History Encyclopedia* May 21, 2014. https://www.ancient.eu/article/687/health-care-in-ancient-mesopotamia/.

[2] Even the monotheistic Hebrews made reference to it as a symbol of healing *vide* Numbers 21:6-8.

[3] Ibid.

[4] "What was Ancient Egyptian Medicine Like?" *Medical News Today* https://www.medicalnewstoday.com/articles/323633.

[5] Ibid.

[6] "Brief History During the Snow Era". *ucla.edu*. Archived from the original on 17 January 2017. Retrieved 1 January 2016.

That said, despite the lack of empirical knowledge, the Egyptian concept of disease and contagion was set in a rather sophisticated view of the cosmos. For the ancient Egyptians, as well as other Middle Eastern societies in antiquity, creation was in a constant state of conflict between *Maat* and *Isfet*. *Maat* represented order and harmony while *Isfet* stood for chaos and discord. Each one eternally sought to overcome the other, and if *Isfet* prevailed, creation – including the gods – would return to the eternal darkness from which it came. *Maat* was personified as a goddess of the same name who ordered the universe, whereas *Isfet* was embodied by the god Set.

The life of the nation revolved around this struggle, and the king in particular was charged with maintaining the fragile balance between the two forces by performing the sacred rituals that ensured that the sun rose every morning. The sun god Ra descended to the underworld every night and there battled terrible monsters, the manifestations of *Isfet*. He could only rise in the morning again, when, with the aid of all Egypt, he overcame their relentless attacks. All existence was a result of the ceaseless struggle between order and chaos, and disease was no exception. Infectious diseases were then treated by *Heka*, the elemental force that created the world, kept it in existence, and allowed the king to maintain the balance between *Maat* and *Isfet*. This force pervaded all of existence and was exercised in medicine by the use of charms, ritualistic formulae and prayers.

The contagions known to have afflicted the ancient Egyptians include smallpox, typhoid, the common cold, tuberculosis, malaria, dysentery and bilharsiasis, a disease spread by contaminated water.[7] To counter these diseases, priests and priestesses invoked such deities as Sekhmet, Serket, Sobek, and Nefertum. Sekhmet was a goddess represented by the head of a lioness and was the cause of plagues as well as their cures. She rejoiced in the titles "Mistress of Dread" and "Lady of Slaughter" and at one time had to be prevented from exterminating all of humanity by Ra. But she had her tender side as well and often heard her devotees pleading for mercy.[8] Her cult was centered in Memphis, where she was invoked as "The Destroyer," but, like most of the members of the Egyptian pantheon, she was devoted to *Maat* and as such was a great protector of Egypt and its people.

---

[7] Joshia J. Mark, "Ancient Egyptian Medicine", *Ancient History Encyclopedia* February 17, 2017. https://www.ancient.eu/Egyptian_Medicine/.

[8] Wilkinson, Richard H. (2003). *The Complete Gods and Goddesses of Ancient Egypt*. Thames & Hudson. p. 181.

An ancient Egyptian engraving of Sekhmet

Every year, the saving of humankind from Sekhmet's plague was commemorated by drinking beer stained with pomegranate juice. Ra satiated Sekhmet's literal lust for blood by offering her red-stained beer, and she drank so much of it that she fell asleep. When she awoke, the first person she saw was Ptah (creation). She fell in love with him instantly and relented of her wrath against the world. Their child was Nefertum, who went into the world with the gift of healing. Needless to say, the Egyptians' prayers to Sekhmet did nothing to actually relieve the horrors of pestilence, but copious amounts of beer, colored or not by pomegranate juice, may have rendered the sufferer insensible to them.

However, one aspect of Egyptian priestly medicine may have done much to prevent the spread of pestilence. Ritual purity was very important to the Egyptians, who were obsessed by cleanliness, so much so that a worshipper could not approach his or her god without washing his body as an exterior expression of their interior purity of intention. All filth and decaying matter had to be removed from the sacred places. As a result, these practices may have inadvertently aided in the containment of contagion, and the sacred precincts to which the sick went might have unintentionally operated as quarantine centers.

When considering plagues and ancient Egypt, readers might instantly think of the famous account of the plagues that struck Egypt as described in Exodus. Most scholars struggle to find any reference to what might be viewed as a historical basis for them, but there is an obscure allusion to the Nile becoming blood dating from around 1250 BCE.[9] In the same vein, attempts have been made to identify two epidemics that the Bible might be referring to, because the sixth plague is described in this way: "And the Lord said to Moses and Aaron: Take to you handfuls of ash out of the chimney, and let Moses sprinkle it in the air in the presence of Pharao. And be there dust upon all the land of Egypt: for there shall be boils and swelling blains both in men and in beasts, in the whole land of Egypt."[10]

Painful boils and swellings are symptomatic of smallpox (*Variola*), and the disease has been known to afflict Egyptian communities as far back as at least 3,000 years ago. An ingenious if unlikely explanation has been offered too for the death of the firstborn of Egypt, suggesting that the red algal brooms conjectured to turn the Nile red released poisonous substances called mycotoxins. These mycotoxins may have contaminated the grain that grew along the riverbanks. As the first children would have been given first place at the table after their parents, it is possible that they tended to get sick and die before their siblings.[11] For now, this is sheer speculation.

The culture whose traditions inflicted such dire plagues upon the Egyptians had a very different worldview and thus a different attitude to disease and plague. In the Hebrew cosmogony, the single deity did not emerge from the primeval chaos as did the gods of Egypt but stood outside of time and space and created the universe. All being was good in itself,[12] but sin disrupted the divine order. Plague and morbidity in general was viewed mainly as sent by the creator to correct this disorder, though just persons might be tried and purified by illness.[13]

Normally, the just man would be protected from pestilence, as expressed in Psalm 91: "There shall no evil befall thee, neither shall any plague come nigh thy dwelling. For he shall give his angels charge over thee, to keep thee in all thy ways."[14]

---

[9] Enmarch, Roland (2011). "The Reception of a Middle Egyptian Poem: The Dialogue of Ipuwer and the Lord of All". In Collier, M.: Snape, S. (eds.) *Ramesside Studies in Honour of K. A. Kitchen*, Rutherford pp. 173–175.

[10] Exodus 9: 8-9 Douay Rheims Bible.

[11] "The Science of the 10 Plagues", Live Science April 11, 2017 https://www.livescience.com/58638-science-of-the-10-plagues.html.

[12] Genesis 1:1-31.

[13] Job 1:13-22.

[14] V. 10-11, King James Version.

A narration in the Second Book of Samuel (chapter 24) illustrates the Hebrews' attitude toward the plague and the response to it. King David wishes to conduct a census of all the inhabitants of Israel but ignores the injunction given by God in Exodus 30:12 ("When you take the sum of the children of Israel after their number, then shall they give every man a ransom for his soul to the Lord, when you number them; that there be no plague among them, when you number them."). An offering in atonement was required in acknowledgement of God's mercy in numbering them amongst his people[15] and a failure to do so was a denial of God's rights over his possession. David is rebuked by God and offered one of three punishments in order to atone: famine, war, or plague. The king chooses plague. God inflicts the punishment and in doing so also gives the remedy. He instructs David to erect an altar and offer sacrifice in atonement. When David does this, the plague ceases. According to the text, 70,000 inhabitants of Israel succumbed to the plague. There is no description of the pestilence and thus no indication of what it might have been.

The plague of leprosy is mentioned a number of times in the Bible, though it would seem that a variety of skin disorders are referred to, not just Hansen's disease.[16] It is worth pointing out here that although leprosy may pass from human to human, the possibility of infection is limited.[17] There were lengthy prescriptions in Hebrew Law concerning those afflicted (Leviticus, chapters 13 and 14), who were considered legally unclean and banished from society. When the sufferer's affliction passed, he washed, shaved his head, and after seven days presented himself to a priest, who offered sacrifice for his cleansing according to an elaborate ritual.[18] Unlike the priests of Egypt, the Hebrew priests did not assist in the healing process – their role was to certify the presence or absence of disease and to offer the prescribed sacrifices.[19]

This is not to suggest that Hebrew theology frowned upon healing illnesses. On the contrary, Yahweh is often referred to as the sole healer of Israel, and physicians were regarded as his instruments and thus never assumed the title *rofe* (healer), which belonged to God alone.[20] Practitioners were probably influenced by the teachings of neighboring countries, particularly Egypt, albeit purged of idolatrous and superstitious content.[21]

Of the 600 precepts of the Law of Israel, 213 concern physical health,[22] and the manifold prescriptions concerning washing, diet, sexual conduct, legal impurity, and social congress

---

[15] Commentaries on Exodus 30:12, *Biblehub* https://biblehub.com/commentaries/exodus/30-12.htm.
[16] Louis Isaac Rabinowitz, "Leprosy", *Encyclopedia Judaica* 2008 https://www.jewishvirtuallibrary.org/leprosy.
[17] *Guidelines for the Diagnosis, Treatment and Prevention of Leprosy.* https://apps.who.int/iris/bitstream/handle/10665/274127/9789290226383-eng.pdf?ua=1: World Health Organization. 2018. pp. xiii.
[18] Leviticus 14.
[19] Rabinowitz.
[20] Samuel Vaisrub, Michael A. Denman, Yaakov Naparstek, and Dan Gilon, "Medicine" *Encyclopedia Judaica* 2008, https://www.jewishvirtuallibrary.org/medicine.
[21] Ibid.
[22] Ibid.

would have done much to prevent or at least hinder the spread of infectious diseases. This was not lost on non-Jews, especially when epidemics were spreading and the Jewish population seemed to be less affected than non-Jewish populations.

Perhaps the most persecuted people in Europe over the centuries were the Jews, and it was no different during the Black Death. Muisis reported, "In 1349, Jews were seized and put in chains and into prison everywhere, in all the places where they dwelt. The reason for this as a strong suspicions that they planned to destroy the Christians by means of poison, and that they had secretly put poison into wells, springs and rivers so that Christians would drink it. And the common report was that they had done this in various places. For there were some among the Jews who were cunning and learned astrologers and they had forecast the impending mortality from the course of the stars, and this encouraged them to put their evil intention into practice with more confidence and cunning. They also saw by the course of the stars that a religious sect was to be destroyed (and they hoped that this meant the Christians) and that men bearing red crosses would appear (and they were unsure whether this meant their sect would then be destroyed); and they said many other things which it would take too long to relate here."

A medieval depiction of Jews being burned in Strasbourg, France

Not only was there an ongoing racial and religious hatred of the people often derisively referred to by Christians as "God's chosen people," but in the case of the Black Death, there seemed to be a rational reason to believe that the Jews were somehow waging a secret war on the Christians. The reason for this assumption was the observation by many that the pestilence did not spread across Jewish communities as much as it did among Gentile ones. What the misled minds did not understand was that the strict dietary and health codes that the Jews observed meant they were living in a much cleaner and healthier environment than their Christian neighbors. Therefore, what seemed to be some sort of conspiracy was actually the result of good hygiene paying off.

Of course, that did not stop Jews from being persecuted. Muisis continued, "Few or no Jews had lived in the kingdom of France since the days of St. Louis; but in other kingdoms and countries where they were to be found they were all arrested and charged ad many denied the accusation but some confessed that that had been their intention. I do not know the truth of what happened in distant countries, but the word was that throughout Germany and in other countries they were burnt, or beheaded, or killed by some other means. And certainly in Lotharingia and Bari all those who could be found were burnt."

Making things worse, when Jewish men and women were arrested, they were often tortured until they confessed, adding fuel to the fire of prejudice. One Jewish man named Agimet was living in Geneva, and after being extensively tortured, he confessed that he was part of a bigger plot by the Jews against the Christians. Under duress, Agimet asserted that a Rabbi by the name of Payret, who lived in Chambery, called him in and told him, "We have been informed that you are going to Venice to buy silk and other wares. Here I am giving you a little package of half a span in size which contains some prepared poison and venom in a thin, sewed leather-bag. Distribute it among the wells, cisterns, and springs about Venice and the other places to which you go, in order to poison the people who use the water of the aforesaid wells that will have been poisoned by you, namely, the wells in which the poison will have been placed."

In the Americas, disease was considered an affliction from the gods as punishment for some transgression, and in Aztec society patients had the advantage of knowing which particular god was chastising them. Minor ailments, however, did not necessarily imply the wrath of the gods and could be treated by the priest-physicians with a variety of herbal preparations. If one suffered from rheumatism or a hangover, he was being punished by Tlaloc (the god of rain, water, and storms) and had to placate the god by offering sacrifice at a sacred river. Xochiquetzal was the goddess of love and beauty and punished those guilty of sexual taboos with venereal disease.

Perhaps not surprisingly, the Aztec believed there were multiple gods responsible for plagues depending on the symptoms exhibited. Those which caused rashes and skin eruptions were sent by Xipe Totec (god of agriculture), who flayed himself in order to feed humankind, much in the same way as maize kernels shed their outer coverings before germinating. The cure was to wear the flayed skin of a human sacrifice in public.[23] Pestilence which caused boils was the work of Xochipilli (the god of arts and games). Those punished by Tezcatlipoca, the chief god, could expect no mercy, and the diseases he sent to punish broken vows were considered incurable.[24]

In the culture of another Mesoamerican people, the Maya, medicine was the exclusive province of sacred practitioners or *ah-men*, who frequently used hallucinogens and other mind-altering substances in order to communicate with the gods and divine the origin of illness. It was believed that disease was caused by the gods possessing the bodies of those who had offended them, and to free the body, it was necessary to communicate with the god by means of altering consciousness and ritual cleansing. Like other societies who had no access to modern science, the Maya extensively employed herbal remedies and compiled a vast amount of knowledge in that area. Unfortunately, both the gods and herbal remedies were powerless in the face of new and deadly diseases that Europeans introduced to the Mesoamericans during the 16th century. A host of Old World diseases including smallpox and bubonic plague, for which the indigenous peoples possessed no immunity, annihilated as much as 95% of the population, with some areas entirely depopulated.[25] In terms of percentages, the mortality rates attributed to the Black Death in the 14th century pale in comparison.

In the ancient Greco-Roman world, illness was also seen as divine punishment, though the gods were not perceived as necessarily just. In fact, the gods were believed to be capricious, with personalities and characteristics quite similar to mortals. They could be undependable, avaricious, vainglorious, conceited, vengeful, and vicious, but they were immortal and had powers over humanity that they often used without justice or mercy. In Hebrew and Egyptian theology, there was a standard of morality by which individuals were judged, but not in Greek and Roman theology. Even in death, mortals that offended the gods could be imprisoned in Tartarus, a wasteland of terror and torment below the Earth. It was there that Crete's King Sisyphus eternally rolled a boulder up a mountain, Tantalus was tortured by food and drink he could never reach, and the giant Tityos was torn alive by vultures over and over again. Those beloved by the gods might be placed in the Elysian Fields at the westernmost edge of the Earth, but the common herd of mortals passed eternity in a realm differing little from earthly existence. The evils sent by the gods might be averted by sacrifices, but only for a time, because the wrathful gods might change their minds just as mortals did.

Plagues and pestilence were associated with Apollo, the god of the sun, light, and knowledge. He was revered as a healer, for just as he unleashed plagues he could cause them to cease. An early reference to his might is to found in *The Iliad,* where Homer wrote of the god shooting

---

[23] Guerra, Francisco (Aug 2012). "AZTEC MEDICINE". *Medical History*. **10** (4): 315–338.

[24] Ibid.

[25] Nunn, Nathan; Qian, Nancy (2010). "The Columbian Exchange: A History of Disease, Food, and Ideas". *Journal of Economic Perspectives*. **24** (2): 163–188.

plague arrows at the Greeks for nine days "with a face as dark as night, and his silver bow rang death as he shot his arrow in the midst of them." Victims of pestilence might visit Apollo's temples and offer sacrifices of expiation.

Asclepius was another god of healing, and he was more approachable than Apollo in that he was more inclined to heal pestilence than inflict it. He was the son of Apollo and a mortal woman named Coronis and thus sympathetic to the plight of weak mortals. He was taught medicine by the centaur Chiron and became a greater healer than even his father. He even learned to raise the dead. Zeus, king of the gods, was so fearful of mortals learning the secret of immortality that he struck Asclepius dead with a thunderbolt. The healer's popularity, however, was so great that Zeus was forced to restore him to life and elevate him to the status of an Olympian god, presumably on the understanding that he would not give the secret of immortality to men.

Michael F. Mehnert's picture of an ancient statue of Asclepius

It is probably no coincidence that the cult of Asclepius grew from the 5th century BC onwards. Plagues broke out in both Italy and Greece in the 430s, and the increased trade between the various Greek colonies scattered about the Mediterranean increased the range of epidemics. Indeed, the first great plagues for which historians have enough material to study date from the period of Hellenic migration. The Plague of Athens, possibly an outbreak of typhus, killed 75,000-100,000 people across Greece from 429-426 BCE.[26] 44 years later, an epidemic –

[26] Papagrigorakis, Manolis J.; Yapijakis, Christos; Synodinos, Philippos N.; Baziotopoulou-Valavani, Effie (2007). "DNA examination of ancient dental pulp incriminates typhoid fever as a probable cause of the Plague of Athens". *International Journal of Infectious Diseases*. **10** (3): 206–214.

possibly influenza – decimated both the Greek and Italian peninsulas.[27]

Asclepius' healing centers, known as Asclepions, were sanctuaries where the ill could seek divine healing from the god. They were temple complexes managed by priests, a throwback to the Egyptian concept of the priest-physician. Suppliants were purified by a series of baths, diets, relaxation exercises and sacrifices which might take the form of prayer or gold. They would then enter into a hypnotic sleep probably induced by opium or other hallucinogens. In this state, Asclepius or perhaps one of his daughters – Panacea and Hygienia – would appear to him. A priest would interpret the dream and communicate a diagnosis and a cure.

A picture of the ruins of an Asclepion on the Greek island of Kos

Many grateful individuals left the Asclepions judging by the number of votive offerings left there. Cures may have been spiritual and emotional more than physical, and the power of the placebo effect should not be ruled out. In any case, over 300 Asclepions arose in the Eastern Mediterranean, and there was a famous one in the River Tiber at Rome, but these institutions were for the wealthy only. Most of the populace had to resort to relying on prayer, sacrifice, spells, magic charms, and simple herbal remedies.

The Roman Empire suffered from a debilitating pandemic from 165-180. It is named the Antonine Plague after the dynasty of emperors at the time, and it is also occasionally referred to as the Plague of Galen, after the renowned physician who fruitlessly strove to save its victims.

---

[27] Potter, C. W. (2002). "Foreword". *Influenza*. Elsevier Science. p. vii.

The pestilence was probably smallpox judging from the descriptions given by Galen,[28] of whom more will be discussed in the next chapter. Fatalities are estimated at 5 million, with a mortality rate of 25%.[29] The empire never recovered from the plague, which hastened its decline.[30]

It seemed that even the gods themselves were powerless against this horrendous pestilence, but many in Europe during the Antonine Plague believed that one descended upon the Earth to at least try to help the suffering of mankind. His name was Glycon, a name that was also unknown to the ancient world until one Alexander (c. 105–170), a physician of dubious qualifications in the town of Abonoteichus in Asia Minor, revealed him. Alexander discovered an egg in the foundations of the temple of Asclepius. When he broke the egg, a small snake emerged which, over the course of a week, grew to the size of a man with a human face and long golden hair. Glycon announced himself to be a son of Apollo, and to have come into the world to bring succor to suffering humanity. He deigned only to speak through his prophet Alexander.

Devotion to Glycon rapidly spread beyond Abonoteichus, in part because by this time the plague had broken out and the people were desperate for protection. Snatches of Glycon's oracles were posted on doors to ward off the pestilence, and prayers were inscribed imploring Glycon's protection against the plague. Rutilianus, the governor of Asia, declared himself the protector of the shrine of Glycon and married Alexander's daughter. Even Marcus Aurelius, known as a wise and stoic philosopher, requested an oracle of Glycon to guarantee victory in a particular encounter with the Marcomanni. Glycon told the emperor that victory was assured if two lions were thrown into the Danube. The battle was a disaster, but Alexander had an explanation: the victory Glycon referred to was the victory of the Marcomanni.

Not everyone was enthused about the new god sent to protect them against the pestilence. The satirist and rhetorician Lucian of Samosata (c. 125-180) was scathing in his appraisal of Glycon and his prophet. In his opinion, Alexander was nothing but a quack who had never excelled in the medical arts. Glycon was nothing but an elaborate puppet operated by Alexander, and he demonstrated the god's authenticity by making it speak through pipes. According to Lucian, there was a price attached to each oracle which Alexander preferred from the rich. He only recruited beautiful men below the age of 18 to sing hymns to Glycon in his temple, and many women boasted that they had children by him.

Lucian recounted facing the prophet himself and testing him with deliberately misleading or obscure questions:

> "I asked a single question in each of two scrolls under a different name, 'What
> was the poet Homer's country?' In one case, misled by my serving-man, who had

[28] D. Ch. Stathakopoulos, *Famine and Pestilence in the late Roman and early Byzantine Empire* (2007) 95.
[29] Verity Murphy, "Past pandemics that ravaged Europe*", BBC News* November 7, 2005.
http://news.bbc.co.uk/2/hi/health/4381924.stm.
[30] Niebuhr, *Lectures on the history of Rome* III, Lecture CXXXI (London 1849), quoted by Gilliam 1961:225.

been asked why he came and had said, 'To request a cure for a pain in the side,' he replied: 'Cytmis I bid you apply, combined with the spume of a charger.'

"To the other, since in this case he had been told that the one who sent it enquired whether it would be better for him to go to Italy by sea or by land, he gave an answer which had nothing to do with Homer: 'Make not your journey by sea, but travel afoot by the highway.'

"Many such traps, in fact, were set for him by me and by others. For example, I put a single question, and wrote upon the outside of the scroll, following the usual form: 'Eight questions from So-and-so,' using a fictitious name and sending the eight drachmas and whatever it came to besides. Relying upon the fee that had been sent and upon the inscription on the roll, to the single question: 'When will Alexander be caught cheating?' he sent me eight responses which, as the saying goes, had no connection with earth or with heaven, but were silly and nonsensical every one.

"When he found out about all this afterward, and also that it was I who was attempting to dissuade Rutilianus from the marriage [to Alexander's daughter] and from his great dependence upon the hopes inspired by the shrine, he began to hate me, as was natural, and to count me a bitter enemy. Once when Rutilianus asked about me, he replied: 'Low-voiced walks in the dusk are his pleasure, and impious matings.'

"And generally, I was of course the man he most hated."[31]

Lucian took an intense interest in exposing the charlatan, as he acknowledged himself. He took pains to find out as much as he could about Alexander, admitting that he was an intelligent and gifted individual who had nevertheless abused his gifts. Lucian made no effort to disguise his contempt:

"While he was still a mere boy, and a very handsome one, as could be inferred from the sere and yellow leaf of him, and could also be learned by hearsay from those who recounted his story, he trafficked freely in his attractiveness and sold his company to those who sought it. Among others, he had an admirer who was a quack, one of those who advertise enchantments, miraculous incantations, charms for your love-affairs, 'sendings' for your enemies, disclosures of buried treasure, and successions to estates. As this man saw that he was an apt lad, more than ready to assist him in his affairs, and that the boy was quite as much enamored with his roguery as he with the boy's beauty, he gave him a thorough education and

---

[31] Lucian of Samosata, *Alexander the false prophet* http://www.tertullian.org/rpearse/lucian/lucian_alexander.htm.

constantly made use of him as helper, servant, and acolyte. He himself was professedly a public physician, but, as Homer says of the wife of Thon, the Egyptian, he knew 'many a drug that was good in a compound, and many a bad one,' all of which Alexander inherited and took over. This teacher and admirer of his was a man of Tyana by birth, one of those who had been followers of the notorious Apollonius, and who knew his whole bag of tricks. You see what sort of school the man that I am describing comes from!"[32]

Alexander prophesied that he himself would live 150 years and then be struck down by lightning. As lightning was a sign of Jupiter's wrath, it seemed an especially bizarre prediction to make, and in the end, he died of a gangrenous leg, a fate Lucian seems to have taken some delight in. During his final illness, it was discovered that the prophet had worn a wig, and that he was completely bald.

Nevertheless, the cult of Glycon survived its creator's death. The prophet Alexander was raised to glory as a god and worshiped as a grandson of Asclepius. A coin issued during the reign of Phillip II (r. 238 – 249) bore an image of Glycon.

---

[32] Ibid.

An ancient statue depicting Glycon

Alexander of Abonoteichus made a special point of excluding both Epicureans and Christians from his temple, and it is hard to see either group objecting. One reason for excluding Christians, beside the opprobrium in which they were generally held, may have been that they were in peril of being arrested and their goods despoiled, so the possibility of profiting off of them was diminished. In any case, no Christian would have asked advice from what they would have viewed as false gods, so it is possible that Christians were going to his shrine specifically to denounce him.

In fact, there was a general feeling of hostility toward Christians at this time, with many believing that the gods were punishing them for permitting the followers of Jesus to remain at large. Much the same way Nero blamed the Great Fire of Rome on Christians, the Antonine Plague gave the state authorities an opportunity to address public anxiety, and Marcus Aurelius subsequently seized upon a similar chance to appease the wrath of the populace.

One of the most notable of the Christian persecutions occurred at Lugdunum (Lyon) in Gaul. An imperial decree in 177 forbade the Christian population from frequenting the public spaces such as baths, markets, and the forum, and those who did appear in those places were publicly humiliated or beaten. Even those who obeyed the edict were attacked in their homes. One of the accusations against the Christians was that they were cannibals, based on a misunderstanding of the belief that the bread they shared in their worship gatherings was the body of Christ.[33] Finally, the city authorities arrested all the Christians, had them brought to the forum, and then imprisoned them. The governor of the province then arrived to judge the case. It is not clear what the legal charges, if any, were, but the 48 Christians were accused of cannibalism and incest (probably based on a misinterpretation of the Christians' mandate to love one another). They were instructed in no uncertain terms to recant and abandon their pernicious faith. Those Christians who refused to do so were imprisoned and tortured.

Some Christians, such as their bishop Pothinus, about 90 years old, died during the torture. Others refused to recant and were thrown into the city amphitheater to be torn to pieces by wild animals. This *Damnatio ad bestias* ("condemnation to the beasts") was a favored method of execution for Christians first used by Nero in 64 CE, and it was a spectacle popular with the general populace. The condemned would be tied to poles before starved lions, bears, leopards, or wolves. If they survived a first attack, they would be presented for a second, or they would subsequently be slain by gladiators. Despite the threat of this awful fate, not one of the Christians thrown in the arena recanted.

It seems that the governor of Lugdunum had written to Marcus Aurelius seeking direction as to how to proceed, and the emperor replied by giving the order to execute the prisoners.[34] The emperor also gave his consent to the beheading of six Christians in Carthage in 180. Similar persecutions occurred throughout the empire.

It seems that these persecutions, while appeasing many of the emperor's subjects, also had an opposite effect. It drew attention to the Christians, who, it was observed, cared for their own, especially those who were poor or ill. They generally remained courageous in adversity without being hateful, and while others fled the plague, they often remained to tend the sick. The belief that they would live on after death provided strength and serenity in the face of death, whether it be from the pestilence or from the state, and as a result the Christian movement grew.[35] The majority of the Roman population viewed this as one might regard the spread of a rodent infestation, but in time Rome would look to Christianity for its salvation.

Miasma and Humors

The idea that diseases were an affliction from the gods was a powerful one and remains so in some quarters, but 500 years before the elite of the Roman Empire offered coins for the oracles

---

[33] Justin Martyr, *First Apology* LXVI.
[34] Michael Grant (2016) *The Antonines: The Roman Empire in Transition*, Routledge p.46.

[35] John Horgan (2019) "Antonine Plague", *Ancient History Encyclopedia* https://www.ancient.eu/Antonine_Plague/

of Glycon, one of the finest minds of the Greek world had already proposed a natural explanation for the morbidities with which humans were afflicted.

Hippocrates, who was born around 460 BCE and died near 370 BCE, was neither a priest nor a prophet, but a physician who had separated medicine from theology. Often called the "Father of Medicine,"[36] Hippocrates held that illness was not a punishment from the gods but the product of factors concerning environment, diet, and behavior.

The attitude toward human affliction exhibited by Hippocrates and his students was certainly an advance from sorcery and divine expiation, but his methods were not based on science as people today would understand it. The concept of science as the construction and organization of a body of knowledge based on testable theories simply did not exist at the time.[37] But there was already a rich tradition of philosophy, which differs from science in that it attempts to arrive at knowledge of matter, being, and ethics by rational argument rather than from empirical evidence. The scope of philosophy, which concerns itself with the whole of existence, is much broader than science, which confines its conclusions to the observable world. Therefore, the medicine of Hippocrates would have treated the patient holistically, meaning physically, emotionally, spiritually, and existentially.

Hippocrates and other Greco-Roman physicians were limited by their lack of knowledge of human anatomy because the dissection of corpses was considered disrespectful to the gods who had created humankind, but they believed they knew enough to effectively treat their patients. They held the doctrine of Νόσων φύσεις ἰητροί, or in Latin *Vis medicatrix naturae*, meaning "the healing power of nature." The body possessed the power to heal itself and the physician simply aided the patient in his recovery and ensured there were no obstacles. The emphasis was on prognosis rather than diagnosis, for if the body was healing itself, knowing the illness was in a sense unnecessary.[38]

Hippocrates ascribed the spread of contagion such as smallpox, influenza, measles, and typhus to *miasma* (literally, "pollution") or foul air. Miasma was supposed to arise from decaying organic matter and infect its victims as it drifted, and it was identifiable by its noxious smell. The theory had a certain logical coherence since pestilence was observed to break out in locations where there was poor hygiene and sanitation, but it also infected seemingly clean areas. It made sense then to suppose that the rotting matter had befouled the air, which in turn had moved to another location. Physicians urged that outbreaks be prevented by ensuring good sanitation, a measure which no modern medico would disagree with, but the ancient physicians believed that

---

[36] "Hippocrates". *Microsoft Encarta Online Encyclopedia*. Microsoft Corporation. 2006. Archived from the original on 2009-10-29.

[37] Lehoux, Daryn (2011). "2. Natural Knowledge in the Classical World". In Shank, Michael; Numbers, Ronald; Harrison, Peter (eds.). *Wrestling with Nature: From Omens to Science*. Chicago: University of Chicago Press. p. 39.

[38] *Garrison, Fielding H. (1966), History of Medicine, Philadelphia: W.B. Saunders Company*, pp.93–94.

once it had broken out, the air might be purified with sweet-smelling herbs, spices, incense or unguents. This idea persisted both in the West and the East until the latter half of the 19th century, and even today the number of households using "air fresheners" and "purifiers" testifies to its persistence.

Hippocrates believed miasma produced disease in the body by causing an imbalance in its humors. Humorism was another medical doctrine of Hippocrates based on philosophy. It rested on the belief of the ancients – notably the Babylonians, Greeks, and the Vedic Indians – that the material elements of the cosmos were air, fire, earth, and water, and that all matter, including the human body, was composed of a balance of the four. The manner in which they balanced might be determined by their properties. Air was hot and wet (as a vapor), fire was hot and dry, earth was cold and dry, and water was of cold and wet. The elements in the body corresponded to four fluids or humors: blood, yellow bile, black bile and phlegm. Blood, being hot and wet, represented air. Yellow bile (the fluid produced by the liver, stored in the gall bladder and sometimes vomited when ill) was supposed to be warm and dry like fire. Black bile (bloody fluid) corresponded to cold and dry earth while phlegm was cold and wet. One's dominant temperament was determined by the balance of fluids and we still use the language of the humors to describe an individual's disposition: sanguine, choleric, melancholic and phlegmatic.

An excess of any of these humors in the body was indicative of an imbalance, and the physician's role was to aid the restoration of balance, so every disease was identified with the excess of a particular humor. In the case of the Antonine Plague, which was probably smallpox, the great Roman physician Galen identified the symptoms with skill and precision, noting erupting ulcers all over the body, the coughing up of *ephelis* (small scabs), and the ulceration of the pharynx, esophagus, and trachea. Modern medicine would recognize these all as clear symptoms of smallpox, and the fact that a physician as educated, skilled, and widely traveled as Galen did not recognize the disease heavily suggests that smallpox was as yet unknown to the Mediterranean world. Galen speculated that the disease was caused by an excess of bile on account of the vomiting of dry blood and the eruption of skin pustules. Bile was considered the most pernicious of the humors,[39] and Galen never arrived at what he might have considered a cure.

In light of the humor theory, Galen's approach to the pestilence hinged on him being able to identify the imbalance of fluids in the bodies of the victims. In other words, he had to determine which humor predominated in those afflicted. Galen wrote extensively about the symptoms of plague victims, but not much about the treatment. The vomiting of dry blood (thought to be bile) and eruption of pustules described by Galen permit the speculation that the disease was caused by an excess of bile, and indeed, bile was considered the most noxious of the humors.[40] Humorist

---

[39] Amir Arsalan Afkhami (2012)"Humoralism" *Encyclopedia Iranica*
    http://www.iranicaonline.org/articles/humoralism-1
[40] Amir Arsalan Afkhami (2012) "Humoralism"*Encyclopaedia Iranica*

theory held that all the humors were present in the blood, so to aid the release of harmful humors, physicians often made an incision to allow blood to drain. This practice, known as bloodletting, was not believed to be dangerous if controlled, as Galen believed that blood was formed in the liver and did not circulate. Despite the fact it didn't work (and often hurt the patient), bloodletting would be practiced well into the 19th century.

Diet was considered the first avenue to restoring the balance of the humors. The adage "you are what you eat" struck especially true for the ancient physician, who believed that certain foods could augment or counter the effects of particular humors. Yellow bile was associated with high temperatures and dryness, black bile with coldness and dryness, phlegm with wet and cold, and blood with heat and moisture. As a result, an excess of black bile might then be treated with foods considered hot, such as garlic, onions, meat and olives.

The emphasis on an appropriate diet probably helped a lot of ill persons, albeit in a somewhat inadvertent and haphazard way. For example, the prescription of only clear, unpolluted water (mountain water was the best)[41] would have not only been beneficial to the patient, but would have assisted in the prevention of contagion, though physicians didn't know the real reasons why.

In the end, Galen was unable to stem the tide of the pestilence, but he could predict the outcome of the disease, noting that all who developed a black rash usually survived. The few notes that survive indicate that he paid great attention to the observation of the symptoms and to reason, and though his philosophical principles were erroneous, his commonsense approach and empathy must surely have provided some relief and comfort to many suffering from the disease.

In fact, the word of Galen on any medical subject was considered so unassailable that his ideas survived well into the 19th century, even though scientific discoveries had raised doubts dating all the way back to the Renaissance. Echoes of humorism survive in modern language, such as when an individual speaks of someone in a "bad humor," and in the use of the terms sanguine, choleric, melancholic and phlegmatic. Many of the elements of humorism, particularly concerning diet, environment, and balance, persist in the realm of alternative medicine.[42]

In Eastern societies, the concept of the material elements was likewise the basis for medicine. The *Ayurveda* system, developed in India during the 2nd century BCE, added a fifth element, ether, which had no observable qualities. As in the West, traditional Ayurveda practitioners placed great emphasis on balance and diet.

---

http://www.iranicaonline.org/articles/humoralism-1
[41] David K. Osborn (2008) "Diet" Food and drink" *Greek Medicine.net*
http://www.greekmedicine.net/hygiene/Diet_Food_and_Drink.html
[42] Chase Breimeier, "The emergence of modern humoralism", *Frontiers: Washing University Review of Health* April 28, 2018 https://frontiersmag.wustl.edu/2018/04/28/the-emergence-of-modern-humoralism/.

Chinese philosophy and medicine was also based on five elements or phases: fire, water, wood, metal, and earth.[43] These were used to explain the body's organs, physical activities, and morbidities. In the 2nd century BCE, elemental theory was incorporated into *Ying-Yan* philosophy, which taught that the cosmos was a whole consisting of contrary but complementary phenomena. As Ying and Yang governed everything, including space and time, the hour at which a patient took a remedy and the place where they took it was often important. A medical journal in 1911 reported a Chinese remedy for the plague: "On the sixth day of the sixth moon gather "Horse Tooth Vegetables" [purslane], dry them in the sun and lay away until New Year's morning, boil until done, and pickle in brine and vinegar for one year. Partaking of this will … prevent the current malady."[44]

Other cures for the plague included the drinking of boiled turnip juice on a specified day, water into which black beans had been cast, and wearing a horse bone wrapped in red cloth on ones side (a woman had to wear it on the right, a man on the left).[45]

Dealing with the Bubonic Plague

In the year 536, the Byzantine Empire, with Constantinople as its capital, was at the height of its glory. It dominated the Mediterranean, as the Roman Empire had in the past, and it had recently reconquered Italy. In this renewed empire, the cult of the ancient gods had been swept away and replaced by the worship of a single deity who had become a man to save humanity. The empire was rich, cultured, and powerful, and Emperor Justinian I (r. 527–565) had greater plans for it yet.

---

[43] Dr Zai, J. *Taoism and Science: Cosmology, Evolution, Morality, Health and more*. Ultravisum, 2015.
[44] "Chinese remedies for the plague", *US National Library of Medicine*
    https://www.ncbi.nlm.nih.gov/pmc/articles/PMC2332311/?page=1.
[45] Ibid.

A contemporary mosaic depicting Justinian I

However, that year a dreadful omen descended over Europe when a dark veil fell upon the sun. While Earth was not completely plunged into darkness, the lack of sunlight caused temperatures to drop and crops to fail. There was snow in summer, and millions died of starvation and cold. This bizarre phenomenon lasted three years and affected not just Europe, but the whole northern hemisphere. Experts postulate it was caused by volcanic dust, possibly from an eruption of Krakatoa,[46] but regardless of how it happened, it initiated a miniature ice age, and while there was certainly a scientific explanation, most medieval people viewed it as a sign of impending doom and the wrath of God. Indeed, the cooler temperatures and wetter summers would have encouraged an increase in the rat population, and rats carried fleas bearing deadly bacteria.

Around the end of spring in 541, a merchant ship from Pelusim in the Nile Delta sailed into the Golden Horn (the inlet between Constantinople and the suburb of Galata) from the Sea of Marmara and docked in the harbor, where the walls of the city extended into the sea. The ship was carrying corn, upon which Constantinople's massive population and people in the empire's other large cities depended. When the ship arrived, some of the seamen on board were ill and

---

[46] Wohletz 2000

exhibiting unusual symptoms, such as painful swelling of the neck, armpits, or groin. They also complained of high fevers and muscle cramps. Much to the horror of onlookers, some vomited blood, while the flesh of others' extremities had turned black. In time, horrible swelling resembling massive boils began to break, with pus and blood pouring out. The affected sailors died within a few days.

Within a week, further outbreaks of the horrific disease occurred, first among merchants, sailors, and dock laborers. After that, it appeared among the general population, and since it seemed to affect beggars, bishops, finely-robed noblemen, and women equally, it seemed that no gender or class would be spared.

The climate around the time of the outbreak was marked by below-average temperatures, damaging crops and causing famine. This meant that people would have migrated throughout the empire in search of food and better agricultural land. It would have also meant an increased reliance on grain imports from Egypt, both of which were favourable to the rapid spread of the pestilence.

Once infected, a victim had but a few days to live. Some might survive a week, but only a very few recovered entirely. The plague was not selective; the hale and hearty, along with the frail and weak, were struck suddenly down with the slimmest of chance for survival. People, as well as livestock, were affected by the disease.

Soon, the plague spread to major trading cities in the eastern Mediterranean, including Antioch and Alexandria. From there, it spread through North Africa, the Balkans, Italy, and Spain. It infected Francia (the kingdom of the Franks), the British Isles, Germany, the Eurasian Steppes, and Persia, following trade routes and inexorably following populations fleeing the pestilence. Provincial trade routes connected with the coast, inland towns, and rural regions were not spared.

Based on the symptoms, physicians and historians believe that Justinian's Constantinople had been introduced to bubonic plague, the same horrific malady that would later be referred to as the Black Death when it struck Europe in the 14th century. Caused by the bacterium *Yersinia pestis,* it is transmitted by fleas on rats and came from the Orient. DNA samples of inert bacterium taken from a victim in Germany indicates that the 541 strain originated somewhere in the Tian Shan Mountains of Central Asia.[47] The Silk Road, the major trading route between Europe and Asia, passed through these ranges, so the strain carried by those sailors in Constantinople had infected Egypt through trade with Ethiopia, which was in touch with merchants from the East.

---

[47] Eroshenko 2017

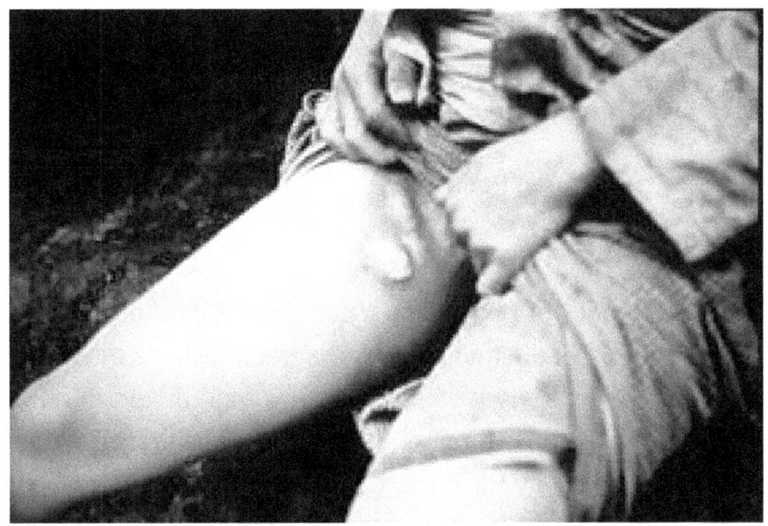

A victim of the plague with swollen lymph nodes visible

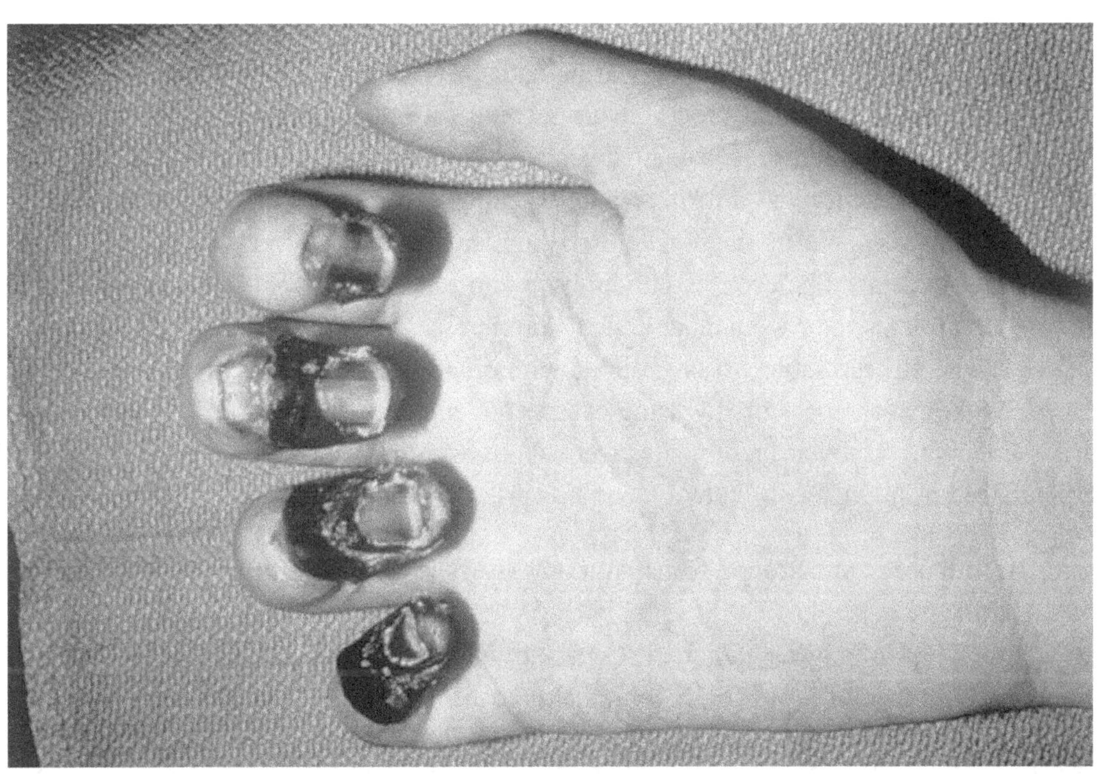

A victim of the plague with fingers blackened by the illness

Galen's advice concerning epidemics was the best and simplest: "Leave quickly, go far away, return slowly."[48] However, most of the threatened population could not flee, and those who did found that the pestilence usually followed anyway. Meanwhile, Byzantine physicians were unfamiliar with the symptoms and thus utterly helpless to deal with the disease.

---

[48] "The Black Death" 2020

There were obvious deficiencies in Byzantine medical theory, but these problems were by no means confined to them, especially taking into account the fact that the state of medicine in the empire was advanced for its time. At first, state hospitals existed for the military and state slaves but not the general public, who were served by the hospitals attached to churches. By the 6th century, however, Byzantine emperors began constructing hospitals for the public alongside those run by the Church.

There were three general grades of physicians: court, public, and private. The physicians of the imperial court were almost always aristocrats, usually given the title of count. Public physicians, employed by the city, were required by law to "honestly attend the poor, rather than basely…serve the rich."[49] Private practitioners were regarded as the worst in the medical profession, for it was widely assumed they treated sick people for material gain alone. The finest physicians in the empire were trained in the famous Medical School of Alexandria, which had been founded in 331 BCE. This was somewhat ironic given that the plague came to Constantinople from Egypt.

The largest hospital in Constantinople was named after St. Pantaleon, a physician and martyr of the 4th century, and as was the case with all hospitals, it filled up quickly. In response to the outbreak, Emperor Justinian canceled subsidies for public doctors and transferred them to the hospitals, which in essence was a form of public healthcare, at least in Constantinople and important urban centers during the plague. Rural inhabitants and the very poor were forced to resort to alternate forms of succor, usually prayers and superstitions. Sufferers sought the touch of the relic of a holy man or woman, and the Church possessed a ceremony for the sick, the *euchelaeon,* whereby the subject was anointed with oil and prayed over. Many reverted to the practices of their pagan ancestors by using charms and amulets. It was probably little consolation for these victims to discover the remedies were about as effective as the expensive "cures" that were purchased from doctors by the rich and powerful.

To be fair to those in and around Constantinople, Europeans wouldn't fare much better when the bubonic plague struck again 900 years later. Due to their limited knowledge of medicine, and the almost total lack of any reliable method of studying and treating disease, there were no verifiable ways known to avoid contracting the disease.

It is estimated that 25-100 million people perished in less than a year.[50] Moreover, outbreaks of the plague continued into the 7th century. Though the Plague of Justinian is much less known than the Black Death that struck Europe in the 14th century, the pestilence in 541 was more intense. Between 1347 and 1351, an estimated 75-200 million died across Europe,[51] but the

---

[49] Rosen 2008:211
[50] Rosen, William (2007). *Justinian's Flea: Plague, Empire, and the Birth of Europe*. Viking Adult. p. 3.
[51] ABC/Reuters (29 January 2008). "Black death 'discriminated' between victims (ABC News in Science)". Australian Broadcasting Corporation. Archived from the original on 20 December 2016. Retrieved 3 November 2008.

Plague of Justinian killed between one third and one half of that amount in the Mediterranean region in the space of just eight months.

When the Black Death hit Europe in the 14th century, Louis Heyligen, a musician serving Cardinal Giovanni Colonna in Italy, hoped that maybe he had learned something while working in the papal court that could save his friends. In a letter, he wrote, "I am writing to you, most dearly beloved, so that you should know in what perils we are now living. And if you wish to preserve yourselves, the best advice is that a man should eat and drink moderately, and avoid getting cold, and refrain from any excess, and above all mix little with people—unless it be with a few who have healthy breath; but it is best to stay at home until the epidemic has passed. According to astrologers the epidemic takes ten years to complete its cycle, of which three have now elapsed, and so it is to be feared that in the end it will have encircled the whole world, although they say that it will affect the cold region more slowly."

On the other hand, Giovanni Boccaccio had his own ideas about what would prevent one from catching the plague, though since he was neither a doctor nor a scientist, his ideas were more of a hopeful collection of rumors going around than any sort of definitive advice. He wrote, "Some thought that moderate living and the avoidance of all superfluity would preserve them from the epidemic. They formed small communities, living entirely separate from everybody else. They shut themselves up in houses where there were no sick, eating the finest food and drinking the best wine very temperately, avoiding all excess, allowing no news or discussion of death and sickness, and passing the time in music and suchlike pleasures. Others thought just the opposite. They thought the sure cure for the plague was to drink and be merry, to go about singing and amusing themselves, satisfying every appetite they could, laughing and jesting at what happened. They put their words into practice, spent day and night going from tavern to tavern, drinking immoderately, or went into other people's houses, doing only those things which pleased them. This they could easily do because everyone felt doomed and had abandoned his property, so that most houses became common property and any stranger who went in made use of them as if he had owned them. And with all this bestial behavior, they avoided the sick as much as possible. … Many others adopted a course of life midway between the two just described. They did not restrict their victuals so much as the former, nor allow themselves to be drunken and dissolute like the latter, but satisfied their appetites moderately. They did not shut themselves up, but went about, carrying flowers or scented herbs or perfumes in their hands, in the belief that it was an excellent thing to comfort the brain with such odors; for the whole air was infected with the smell of dead bodies, of sick persons and medicines."

The flowers or herbs mentioned above were tied together in small bundles called "posies" and may have given rise to a chant later picked up by children. To this day, kids across the world are still familiar with the simple refrain:

"Ring around the rosies

Pocket full of posies

Ashes, ashes

We all fall down."

Although it's impossible to determine with certainty and continues to be debated, many scholars believe the nursery rhyme is a nod to the Black Death. In this seemingly innocuous chant, the first line refers to the bright red cheeks that appeared on the faces of those suffering fever, while the ashes referred to the remains of the burned possessions that had once belonged to the sick. Of course, the dead were the ones who fell down. In support of this interpretation, Peter and Iona Opie, who have long studied nursery rhymes, noted, "The invariable sneezing and falling down in modern English versions have given would-be origin finders the opportunity to say that the rhyme dates back to the Great Plague. A rosy rash, they alleged, was a symptom of the plague, and posies of herbs were carried as protection and to ward off the smell of the disease. Sneezing or coughing was a final fatal symptom, and 'all fall down' was exactly what happened.

While people may have attempted to avoid catching the disease in superstitious but utterly worthless manners, many of those who were well-travelled and well-read in the 14th century noticed that the plague did not seem to manifest itself in the same way everywhere. That may have been because it mutated over time or because there was actually more than one virulent strain going around. The Italian writer Giovanni Boccaccio explained, "The symptoms were not the same as in the East, where a gush of blood from the nose was the plain sign of inevitable death; but it began both in men and women with certain swellings in the groin or under the armpit. They grew to the size of a small apple or an egg, more or less, and were vulgarly called tumors. In a short space of time these tumors spread from the two parts named all over the body. Soon after this the symptoms changed and black or purple spots appeared on the arms or thighs or any other part of the body, sometimes a few large ones, sometimes many little ones. These spots were a certain sign of death, just as the original tumor had been and still remained."

An early 15th century Bible's illustration believed to depict the plague

   Other people believed that the disease came from something people ate. Cortusii Patavini Duo recalled, "Also fish are now not generally eaten, men holding that they have been infected by the infected air. Moreover no kinds of spices are eaten or handled, unless they have been in stock for a year, because men are afraid that they might have come from the galleys of which I spoke. For on many occasions eating fresh spices or certain sea fishes had been found to have extremely unpleasant results."

   For many, the only cause for the illness, or indeed for any type of misfortune, was the wrath of God, but they still commented on the physical conditions of the victims. A monk known as Agnolo di Tura "the Fat" wrote, "[I]n many places in Siena great pits were dug and piled deep with the multitude of dead ... And there were also those who were so sparsely covered with earth that the dogs dragged them forth and devoured many bodies throughout the city. If I am asked what is the cause of pestilence, what is its physical cause and by what means can someone save himself from it, I answer to the first question that sin is the cause. To the second question, I say that it arises from the sea, as the evangelist says: 'There shall be signs in the sun and in the moon and in the stars; and upon the earth distress of nations, by reason of the confusion of the roaring of the sea and of the waves.' For the devil, by the power committed to him when the seas rise up high, is voiding his poison, sending it forth to be added to the poison in the air, and that air spreads gradually from place to place and enters man through the ears, eyes, nose, mouth, pores and other orifices. Then, if the man has a strong constitution, nature can expel the poison through ulcers, and if the ulcers putrefy, are strangled and fully run their course, the patient will be saved, as can be clearly seen. But if the poison should be stronger than his nature, so that his constitution cannot prevail against it, then the poison instantly lays siege to the heart and the patient dies within a short time, without the relief that comes from the formation of ulcers."

The world has been afflicted with three bubonic plague pandemics: the Plague of Justinian, the Black Death of the Middle Ages, and the little-known Third Pandemic, which began in the mid-19th century and killed more than 12 million people, mostly in China and India. Numerous epidemics have occurred in between these, notably the Great Plague of London of 1665/1666, the Great Plague of Vienna in 1679, the 1720 Great Plague of Marseilles and the Persian Plague of 1772.

Until the Third Pandemic, the weapons for fighting bubonic plague remained prayer, superstition, and the medicine of Hippocrates and Galen. The belief that plague was a heavenly punishment remained persistent, and remedies were often aimed at placating divine justice. Pope Gregory I (r. 590–604), set the template in this regard. During the devastating Plague of Rome in 590, Gregory urged his people to do penance for their sins with prayer and fasting, after which he led them in a procession through the city chanting and beseeching God's grace. The *Golden Legend*, a medieval hagiography, describes how the procession was led by an image of the Blessed Virgin Mary, worshippers dropping to the ground even as it wound through the streets.[52] As the supplicants approached the Mausoleum of the Emperor Hadrian they saw the Archangel Michael sheath his sword over the city, upon which the pestilence abated. Thereafter the Mausoleum was referred to as the Castel Sant'Angelo. A statue of the archangel returning his sword to the scabbard can be seen atop the building, which is now a museum.

The litany chanted during that procession is still used in the Catholic Church today. The *Litaniae Sanctorum* ("Litany of the Saints") continues to contain the petition "Spare us from disease, hunger and war." That first prayerful solemnity survives to this day in the form of Rogation Day (from the Latin *rogare*, to ask), which occurs on April 25, the day of the first procession.

Besides turning to God for relief, the people would often pray to the Blessed Virgin Mary and the saints. The mother of Christ was often invoked by the title *Mater Misericordiae* (Mother of Mercy), depicted in art extending her cloak over her supplicants. Sometimes the image would show angels firing plague arrows which would kill all but those beneath Mary's mantle.[53] Communities surviving the plague often erected plague columns in thanksgiving. These

---

[52] Jacobus de Voragine (c. 1260), Ch 46: "Saint Gregory", *The Golden Legend: Readings on the Saints.*
[53] *Magdalena Łanuszka (Feb 24, 2019) "OUR LADY OF THE PLAGUE", POSZTUKIWANIA*
http://en.posztukiwania.pl/.

structures were placed in town squares and piazzas with an image of the Trinity, the Blessed Virgin Mary or some other Christian saint on top.

During plague times, devotion to Saint Sebastian became widespread. Sebastian was a member of the Praetorian Guard during the reign of Emperor Diocletian. In the year 288, during the Christian persecution of Diocletian, it was discovered that he was a Christian, and he was arrested and condemned. He was shot with arrows and left for dead, but he was nursed back to health by a saintly Christian woman, Irene. In restored health, he confronted Diocletian, whereupon he was executed by being clubbed to death.

It seems natural enough that St. Sebastian should have been considered the patron saint of archers and pin-makers, though it is harder to see why he should have become the patron of plague sufferers. Yet from ancient times, pestilence was represented by arrows. They strike suddenly, mercilessly, deeply, and without discrimination. The wrath of Apollo was imagined as arrows flying from his bow and the Old Testament speaks of pestilence as Yahweh's arrows: "And I will heap disasters upon them; I will spend my arrows on them; they shall be wasted with hunger, and devoured by plague and poisonous pestilence."[54]

It was not unusual then that Sebastian should have been associated with the plague. As early as the 7th century he was invoked as "dispeller of the pestilence."[55] By the time of the Black Death in 1347 the cult of Sebastian had spread throughout Europe, but in art he began to be depicted in the company of another saint with miraculous healing powers. This was Roch or Rocco, a poor mendicant who tended victims of the plague in Italy during the Black Death. He fell ill to the plague himself and was expelled from Piacenza, the city where he was ministering. He withdrew into a forest and made himself a hut of boughs and leaves and prepared to die. Then a dog came, bringing him not only food but healing, for after it licked his wounds, he was healed. Roch returned to society only to be thrown into prison (his uncle suspected him of being a spy), where he died in 1327.

The popular *Golden Legend* recounts his divine visitation in captivity: "[A]non an angel brought from heaven a table divinely written with letters of gold into the prison, which he laid under the head of S. Rocke. And in that table was written that God had granted to him his prayer, that is to wit, that who that calleth meekly to S. Rocke he shall not be hurt with any hurt of pestilence." As a result, the saint is often represented in art revealing his leg marked by the reddened buboes characteristic of bubonic plague.

---

⁵⁴ Deuteronomy 32: 23–24.
⁵⁵ Armand P. Gelpi, "Saint Sebastian and the Black Death", Vesalius, IV, 1, 23–30, 1998.

Francesco Rebalta's painting of St. Rocco

The Church does have a special ritual for victims of the plague like for any serious illness. In the Catholic Church, it was called Extreme Unction, now called Anointing of the Sick, and in the Eastern Orthodox Church it is known as Holy Unction. Sacred oil was traced in the sign of the cross on the victim's body and accompanied by prayer for his spiritual comfort and healing. The practice originates from the injunction of the apostle James: "Is any among you sick, let him call for the presbyters of the church, and let them pray over him, anointing him with oil in the name of the Lord; and the prayer of faith will save the sick man, and the Lord will raise him up; and if he has committed sins, he will be forgiven. Therefore, confess your sins to one another and pray for one another, that you may be healed."[56]

The first intended end of this sacrament was the spiritual healing of the sufferer, but it was believed that God might also grant physical healing.[57] The administration of Extreme Unction to the sick, even plague victims, was considered a sacred duty of the clergy, and during the Black Death priests died at a higher rate than most other classes of society. This was because they were constantly moving from house to house and often in a state of physical exhaustion and with little nourishment.[58]

The Catholic Church brought improvements to European society regarding health and medicine, contrary to the prevailing notion that medieval communities lived in abject squalor. Jesus cared for the sick and the poor and instructed his disciples to do likewise. Thus, when the Roman Empire was converted, it maintained public hospitals in the cities, staffed by trained physicians, both male and female,[59] whereas the pre-Christian empire only treated soldiers or slaves in public institutions. Beyond the Romans and Byzantines, healthcare became the province of the clergy and the religious, and monasteries usually maintained facilities for the care of the sick. Clerics and monastics were the best-educated members of medieval society and many were the ablest physicians of their day and easily the equal of those of antiquity. It was natural enough that the care of the sick should be entrusted first to them, in the ancient tradition of the priest-healer acting as the instrument of God. Individuals did place emphasis on personal cleanliness and hygiene, despite often lacking running water, and the Hollywood image of dirty-faced peasants with uncombed hair and no regard for their appearance is undoubtedly incorrect.[60] Everyone habitually washed themselves and their clothes and changed their bedding, which tended to harbor fleas and lice. Fleas just so happened to be carriers of the Bubonic Plague.

In cities and towns, the governing authorities imposed regulations regarding the cleanliness of public places and areas around houses. Also contrary to popular belief, medieval townspeople did not throw their waste – including that of the privy – into the street. This was in fact prohibited, and the town's inhabitants were encouraged to use a communal cesspit. This does mean to say that standards of hygiene were uniformly maintained all the time, since the constant traffic of pack and market animals through the streets, coupled with frequent rain made it difficult to maintain good sanitation and to keep away rodents. The fleas which carried the plague were brought by rats, and the plague went wherever the rats went.

---

[56] James 5:14-16
[57] "Catechism of the Catholic Church, 1532". Vatican.va. Retrieved 2014-07-29.
[58] John Kelly (2006), *The Great Mortality* Harper Perennial New York p. 224.
[59] Miller, Timothy (1985). *The Birth of the Hospital in the Byzantine Empire*. Baltimore, Maryland: Johns Hopkins. pp. 142–146.
[60] Mark Cartwright (December 7, 2018), "Medieval Hygiene", *Ancient History Encyclopedia* https://www.ancient.eu/Medieval_Hygiene/.

Physicians were as helpless in the face of the plague as their predecessors had been during the Plague of Justinian. They often lanced the buboes or swellings on the victims in the belief – based on Galen – that the excess humor should be released in order to restore balance. Needless to say, boil-lancing and bleeding were ineffective, though physicians did realize that allowing too much blood to drain would injure the patient's health.[61] However, it has been suggested that bloodletting may have been beneficial in that it forced patients to rest, thus helping to maximize the chances of recovery (not everyone who contracted the plague died).[62] The only direct treatment for bubonic plague, however, is antibiotics, which did not come into use until the early 20th century.

Regarding diet, physicians counseled against consuming "moist" foods such as milk, fruit and fish. Hot foods were considered beneficial,[63]as well as white bread and wine, and fresh, wholesome food had to be taken in moderation. Many items such as fish, poultry, wine and certainly white bread were generally not available to the poor.

A concoction called theriac was reputed to be the most effective remedy against bubonic plague. It was made of a variety of spices and herbs including rhubarb, saffron, cinnamon, pepper and ginger. There were in fact as many as 80 ingredients, often including opium, and it was very costly to produce since most of its ingredients were considered luxury items.[64]

Another method thought beneficial involved applying a desiccated toad to the sufferer's buboes. Toads were regarded as noxious creatures, and it was supposed that it would absorb the poison from the body.[65] If no toad was available, a viper might serve equally as well.

Overall, physicians favored prevention rather than cure, as they do today, and there were various measures that could be taken. Miasmic air had of course to be avoided, and physicians would advise against going outside at certain times based on the position of the heavenly bodies. Today astrology is regarded by science as sheer superstition but in ancient and medieval times it differed little from what is now called astronomy. It was believed that the celestial bodies influenced the earthly sphere in a purely natural manner. Many scholars followed the opinion of the Dominican cleric and natural philosopher Albert of Cologne (c. 1200–1280), who taught that the conjunction of Jupiter and Mars in Gemini produced conditions conducive to miasmic air, based on the belief that Jupiter was sanguine and Mars choleric.[66] However, when the Black Death passed, Priest Conrad of Megenburg (1309–1374) pointed out that conjunctions lasted

---

[61] Byrne, Joseph P (2004), *The Black Death*, Westport, CT: Greenwood Press pp. 59–61.

[62] Kealey, Edward J. (1981) *Medieval Medicus*, Baltimore, MD: The Johns Hopkins University Press, pp. 4–6.
[63] Byrne p. 48.
[64] Christiane Nockels Fabbri, "Treating Medieval Plague: The Wonderful Virtues of Theriac", Early Science and Medicine 12, No. 3 (January 2007): 248–263.
[65] Ernest B. Gillman," Plague, arsenic and a dried toad", *The Lancet* June 13, 2009.
[66] Albertus Magnus, On the Causes of the Properties of the Elements, trans. Irven M. Resnick Milwaukee, WI: Marquette University Press, 2010), 110, accessed November 3, 2014, ProQuest Ebrary.

only two years, whereas the great pestilence had lasted five.[67]

Some contemporaries proposed other causes beyond decaying organic matter to explain the great pestilence. Some thought that earthquakes allowed miasma from the depths of hell to infect the earth while others believed that southerly winds or sea air caused pestilence.[68] Fires were often lit to purify the noxious air. Here, the infamous persecution of Jews during the Black Death might be mentioned. They were believed to be untouched by the plague and so must be its cause. Jews were ghettoed at the time, and if they were indeed relatively unscathed, their separation from the wider community is probably an explanation.[69] It was widely believed that Jews had poisoned the wells they did not use, and moreover were forbidden to use by separation laws. Thousands of Jews were murdered with many civil authorities turning a blind eye or even abetting their assailants.[70] The popes issued edicts protecting the Jews, but often with little effect.[71]

Medieval doctors knew the plague was contagious, but they obviously had no knowledge of microbiological organisms, and their advice was often simply to flee the area where the plague broke out. Only the well-to-do could afford to do this, and even then the plague invariably followed them due to the rats that always accompany human habitation. Given this pattern, it soon became obvious that everyone who had a sick relative faced a heartrending choice: stay and nurse that person and likely catch the disease or leave a loved one to die alone and have a chance to live. Cortusii Patavini Duo explained, "The wife fled the embrace of a dear husband, the father that of a son, and the brother that of a brother. Even the houses or clothes of the victims could kill. Those burying, carrying, seeing or touching the infected often died suddenly themselves. Just as one infected sheep infects the whole flock, so one death within a household was always followed by the death of all the rest, right down to the dogs. The bodies even of noblemen lay unburied. Many, at a price, were buried by poor wretches, with priests or candles. Indeed in Venice, where 100,000 died, boats were hired at great expense to carry bodies to the islands and the city was virtually deserted."

It was unquestionably a shocking thing to see and experience across Europe, and it inevitably led to communities falling apart at the seams. People now warily kept their distance from friends and walked out on the families that they had been completely devoted to just weeks before. At the same time, however, even those who may have desired to escape often didn't have the means to actually leave, something Boccaccio remarked on when he wrote, "The plight of the lower and most of the middle classes was even more pitiful to behold. Most of them remained in their houses, either through poverty or in hopes of safety, and fell sick by thousands. Since they received no care and attention, almost all of them died. Many ended their lives in the streets both

---

[67] Byrne, p. 42.
[68] Byrne, p. 42–43.
[69] "The Black Death", *Jewish History.org*, https://www.jewishhistory.org/the-black-death/.
[70] Howard N. Lupovitch (2009), *Jews and Judaism in world history* p. 92.
[71] Simonsohn, Shlomo (1991). *Apostolic See and the Jews*. Toronto: Pontifical Institute of Mediaeval Studies, Vol. 1: Documents, 492. p. 1404.

at night and during the day; and many others who died in their houses were only known to be dead because the neighbors smelled their decaying bodies. Dead bodies filled every corner. Most of them were treated in the same manner by the survivors, who were more concerned to get rid of their rotting bodies than moved by charity towards the dead. With the aid of porters, if they could get them, they carried the bodies out of the houses and laid them at the door; where every morning quantities of the dead might be seen. They then were laid on biers or, as these were often lacking, on tables."

Witnessing these kinds of choices being made, Boccaccio noted, "Such fear and fanciful notions took possession of the living that almost all of them adopted the same cruel policy, which was entirely to avoid the sick and everything belonging to them. By so doing, each one thought he would secure his own safety." Not surprisingly, this led to a complete breakdown among families and communities. He continued, "Others again held a still more cruel opinion, which they thought would keep them safe. They said that the only medicine against the plague-stricken was to go right away from them. Men and women, convinced of this and caring about nothing but themselves, abandoned their own city, their own houses, their dwellings, their relatives, their property, and went abroad or at least to the country round Florence, as if God's wrath in punishing men's wickedness with this plague would not follow them but strike only those who remained within the walls of the city, or as if they thought nobody in the city would remain alive and that its last hour had come. … One citizen avoided another, hardly any neighbor troubled about others, relatives never or hardly ever visited each other. Moreover, such terror was struck into the hearts of men and women by this calamity, that brother abandoned brother, and the uncle his nephew, and the sister her brother, and very often the wife her husband. What is even worse and nearly incredible is that fathers and mothers refused to see and tend their children, as if they had not been theirs."

Moreover, given the widespread belief that people could die at any time, a real sense developed among them that there was no sense in maintaining normal customs or routines. As such, there were not enough hands or will to plant and tend crops, and many field lay fallow. Likewise, there was no need to make cloth or clothes, since there was no one around to buy or wear them. Funeral shrouds might have been big business, but no one was willing to go near a dead body to dress it.

As is often the case, when families fell apart, those in the community were forced to pick up the slack and provide care for the dying. However, the job was so terrible and so likely to be deadly that only the best or worst sort of people in the community were willing to do it. This led, at least in the minds of some, to a breakdown in the morals of society; while monks and nuns from abbeys across the continent came to help, Boccaccio claimed that people who saw no chance in survival gave in to vices and urges that would've previously been unthinkable: "Thus, a multitude of sick men and women were left without any care, except from the charity of friends (but these were few), or the greed, of servants, though not many of these could be had even for high wages, Moreover, most of them were coarse-minded men and women, who did little more than bring the sick what they asked for or watch over them when they were dying. And very often these servants lost their lives and their earnings. Since the sick were thus abandoned by neighbors, relatives and friends, while servants were scarce, a habit sprang up which had never been heard of before. Beautiful and noble women, when they fell sick, did not scruple to take a young or old man-servant, whoever he might be, and with no sort of shame, expose every part of their bodies to these men as if they had been women, for they were compelled by the necessity of their sickness to do so. This, perhaps, was a cause of looser morals in those women who survived."

While Boccaccio's observation in that regard was almost certainly colored by strict social codes, one of the most important aspects of the Black Death is that it did not discriminate by class. The notion that rich people were just as likely to be victims as poor people was shocking to Europeans, especially since there were guidelines governing how and with whom people interacted.

No matter the case, those obliged to remain were counseled to burn sweet-smelling substances such as scented wood and incense. Rosewater, amber, aloes and Eau de Cologne were also useful to have in the house, though again, these were items that usually only the wealthy would have. Faces were masked with cloths or masks and the beak-like headgear of the "plague doctors," filled with aromatic herbs are of course iconic. These beaks, along with the long waxed robes, gloves and wide-brimmed hats, were part of a uniform that became common from the 1630s.[72]

---

[72] Christine M. Boeckl, *Images of plague and pestilence: iconography and iconology* (Truman State University Press, 2000), pp. 15, 27.

A contemporary engraving of a plague doctor

Juan Rivas' picture of a plague doctor's outfit

This came at a time when medical care was no longer the exclusive realm of the clergy or even of the educated. In fact, several plague doctors had little experience of medicine at all,[73] many being failed physicians or young doctors hoping to establish a practice. Sometimes they had absolutely no medical experience, and it is known in one case that a certain plague doctor had been a fruit seller.[74] They were paid by the towns which sent for them and thus did not distinguish between poor and rich.[75] It can only be imagined that the pay must have been considerable, for it is difficult to imagine the attraction of a profession that exposed a person to death on a daily basis.

Nonetheless, there were many dedicated plague doctors, one of the most famous being Michel

---

[73] Cipolla, Carlo M. (1977). "The Medieval City". In Miskimin, Harry A. (ed.). *A Plague Doctor*. Yale University Press. p. 64.

[74] Byrne, p. 170.

[75] Cipolla, p. 68.

de Nostradame, otherwise known as Nostradamus (1503–1566). He was a qualified physician and astrologer as well as an occultist and seer. His commonsense preventative measures included removing rotting matter and nearby corpses, ventilating dwellings, and the drinking of plenty of clean water. He also recommended the consumption of rose hip tea,[76] an excellent source of Vitamin C which is important for body repair and immune system function.[77] He acted against most of his contemporaries in refusing to bleed his patients. Incidentally, recent reports that Nostradamus predicted the COVID-19 pandemic and predicted that it would destroy the world are utterly false.

It might be imagined that the best plague physicians were those who were compassionate and soothing and capable of alleviating at least some of the agony. More cynical assessments of a doctor's qualifications abounded, such as that of the French chronicler Jean Froissart (c. 1337–c. 1405), who wrote, "Doctors need three qualifications: to be able to lie and not get caught; to pretend to be honest; and to cause death without guilt."[78]

During this time, medical theory in Muslim lands was based on the teachings of Hippocrates and Galen, as in the West, but its marriage to Islamic theology elicited a somewhat different response. It was not generally viewed as a sign of the wrath of God but rather as a mercy offering the opportunity of martyrdom to believers.[79] According to tradition, the prophet Mohammed said that if plague "is in a land do not approach it, but if it occurs in a land while you are there, do not leave to escape it."[80] According to Islamic theology, everything is in the hands of God, so it was supposed that an individual would only be infected if God commanded it. Thus, Islamic physicians tended to dismiss the danger of contagion, though there were still some reputable doctors who asserted that the plague could be transmitted.

Even in the midst of the worst plague that had ever hit Europe, many people remained optimistic in part by keeping the faith, as noted by Gilles li Muisis: "While the mortality was at its height an enormous number of people including those of noble birth, knights, matrons, ecclesiastics, canons and members of religious orders, as well as ordinary men and women flocked to the monastery of St. Peter at Hennegau, when it was discovered that there were relics of St. Sebastian in a shrine there. Their devotion was wonderful to behold, but as the mortality began to abate after the feast of All Saints the pilgrimages and devotion ceased. While the pestilence raged in France pilgrims of both sexes and every social class also poured from all parts of France into the monastery of St. Medard at Soissons, where the body of that martyr St. Sebastian was said to lie. But when the disaster came to an end, the pilgrimage and devotion

---

[76] Pickover, Clifford A., *Dreaming the Future: The fantastic story of prediction*, Prometheus Books, 2001, p. 279.
[77] "Vitamin C". *Dietary Reference Intakes for Vitamin C, Vitamin E, Selenium, and Carotenoids*. Washington, DC: The National Academies Press. 2000. pp. 95–185.
[78] "Cures for the Black Death" *BBC Bitesize* https://www.bbc.co.uk/bitesize/guides/z7r7hyc/revision/4.
[79] Lawrence I. Conrad "Tāʿūn and Wabāʾ Conceptions of Plague and Pestilence in Early Islam", Journal of the Economic and Social History of the Orient 25, No. 3 (1982): 271–272. 123.
[80] Robert Fisk, "Iran's Coronavirus outbreak is bizarrely reminiscent of the Black Death", *Independent* February 27, 2020.

ended too."

As a result, the Flagellant Movement reached its height during the Black Death.[81] They processioned through the streets of the town bare-chested and scourged their backs with whips in penance for the sins that had supposedly brought the wrath of God upon the people. In 1349, Robert of Avesbury wrote the following eyewitness account:

> "In that same year of 1349, about Michaelmas (September 29) over six hundred men came to London from Flanders, mostly of Zeeland and Holland origin. Sometimes at St Paul's and sometimes at other points in the city they made two daily public appearances wearing cloths from the thighs to the ankles, but otherwise stripped bare. Each wore a cap marked with a red cross in front and behind.

> "Each had in his right hand a scourge with three tails. Each tail had a knot and through the middle of it there were sometimes sharp nails fixed. They marched naked in a file one behind the other and whipped themselves with these scourges on their naked and bleeding bodies.

> "Four of them would chant in their native tongue and, another four would chant in response like a litany. Thrice they would all cast themselves on the ground in this sort of procession, stretching out their hands like the arms of a cross. The singing would go on and, the one who was in the rear of those thus prostrate acting first, each of them in turn would step over the others and give one stroke with his scourge to the man lying under him.

> "This went on from the first to the last until each of them had observed the ritual to the full tale of those on the ground. Then each put on his customary garments and always wearing their caps and carrying their whips in their hands they retired to their lodgings. It is said that every night they performed the same penance."[82]

The Catholic Church never approved of the movement, and after its members began to dissociate itself from the official hierarchy, it was condemned. Nevertheless, public flagellants came to be tolerated in countries such as Spain and Italy as long as the Church's authority was acknowledged.

---

[81] Lewis-Stempel, John (2006). *England: The autobiography: 2,000 years of English history by those who saw it happen*. London: Penguin. p. 76.

[82] Robert of Avesbury: E.M. Thompson (ed), Robertus de Avesbury de Gestis Mirabilbus Regis Edwardi Tertii, Roll Series 1889; Cohn, Norman, The Pursuit of the Millennium: Revolutionary Millenarians and Mystical Anarchists of the Middle Ages (1970).

Germm Theory

Somewhat incredibly, the idea that diseases might be spread by microscopic pathogenic particles was first proposed as far back as the 5th century BCE. The historian Thucydides (c. 460–c. 400 BCE) postulated the existence of spores or *semina* (seeds) that could travel through the air.[83] The Roman scholar Marcus Terrentius Varro (116–27 BCE) went further, coming extraordinarily close to present knowledge by claiming that "there are bred certain minute creatures which cannot be seen by the eyes, which float in the air and enter the body through the mouth and nose and there cause serious diseases."[84]

Unfortunately, these ideas remained mere speculation and were all but ignored by medicine until the invention of the microscope in the 17th century, and even then the correlation between microscopic organisms and illness was not proved, though there was plenty of speculation. In the middle of the 19th century, the English physician John Snow (1813–1858) demonstrated, at least to the satisfaction of a London council during an 1854 cholera outbreak, that the pestilence was not caused by miasma but by biological agents. However, it was left to Louis Pasteur (1822–1895) and Robert Koch (1843–1910) to prove beyond doubt that microorganisms were the cause of infectious diseases such as bubonic plague, cholera, typhus, influenza, measles, and smallpox. Miasma theory had finally been vanquished by germ theory.

---

[83] Singer, Charles and Dorothea (1917) "The scientific position of Girolamo Fracastoro [1478–1553] with especial reference to the source, character and influence of his theory of infection", *Annals of Medical History*, **1**: 1–34.

[84] Varro, Marcus Terentius with Lloyd Storr-Best, trans., *Varro on Farming* (London, England: G. Bell and Sons, Ltd., 1912), Book 1, Ch. XII, p. 39.

Snow

Pasteur

Edward Jenner (1749–1823) had famously demonstrated that immunity to smallpox could be acquired by inoculating persons with a small quantity of cowpox, and this was in the 1760s, long before germ theory had been proved. In the 1880s, Pasteur made discoveries that led to the development of a vaccine against anthrax, leading in turn to a cascade of research that resulted in the prevention of diphtheria, mumps, measles, polio, and other morbidities. In 1897, the first vaccine for bubonic plague was developed, and 2019 saw the introduction of a vaccine against Ebola.[85] As a result, most of the microbial diseases that historically afflicted the human race have

[85] "Merck's Ervebo [Ebola Zaire Vaccine (rVSVΔG-ZEBOV-GP) live] Granted Conditional Approval in the European Union" (Press release). Merck. 11 November 2019.

a vaccine, and plagues which used to decimate populations such as smallpox and cholera are no longer the cataclysmic threats they used to be.

Needless to say, the development of antibiotics since the early 20th century are greatly beneficial in curing many infectious diseases, but they are only effective against bacterial ones such tetanus, typhoid fever and diphtheria.[86] They are not effective in treating viral infections such as influenza and Coronavirus. Indeed, though antiviral treatments exist for some viral infections, for others, treatment merely involves the management of symptoms.[87] With regard to Coronavirus, health experts the world over have emphasized that until a vaccine is produced, there is no way to prevent its spread beyond maintaining personal hygiene, including washing hands, avoiding touching the face, and social distancing. The World Health Organization has taken great pains to emphasize that the following are not proven treatments against Coronavirus:

- Exposing oneself to the sun or to temperatures above 25 degrees Celsius
- Exposing oneself to the cold
- Frequent alcohol consumption
- Exposing oneself to ultraviolet light
- Eating garlic
- Swimming in chlorinated water[88]

Researchers believe a vaccine will be available to the general public by the end of 2021, but even when it's ready, the challenge of immunizing the global population will be colossal. Many of the companies involved in the research simply do not have the capacity to produce vaccines in the quantities required,[89] not to mention the logistical problems of distributing the vaccine to billions of people. Governments and non-governmental organizations (NGOs) are working on these challenges, even as there is still much about the current pandemic that remains unknown.

Enormous strides have been made in disease prevention and treatment in the last 200 years, and the most notorious pestilences that once laid whole civilizations low seem to have been tamed. As recently as September 2018, the Global Preparedness Monitoring Board, an NGO whose avowed purpose was to "monitor progress, identify gaps and advocate for sustained, effective work to ensure global preparedness,"[90] warned of "a very real threat of a rapidly

---

[86] *Antibiotics Simplified*. Jones & Bartlett Publishers. 2011. pp. 15–17.

[87] "Antiviral Medication and Other Treatment" *Viral Infections: Type, Treatment and Prevention*, OnHealth
https://www.onhealth.com/content/1/viral_infections.

[88] Coronavirus disease (COVID-19) advice for the public: Myth busters, *World Health Organization*
https://www.who.int/emergencies/diseases/novel-coronavirus-2019/advice-for-public/myth-busters.

[89] Ibid.

[90] World Health Organization (September 10, 2018) "Global Preparedness Monitoring Board convenes for the first

moving, highly lethal pandemic of a respiratory pathogen killing 50 to 80 million people."[91] As
the Coronavirus began to spread with indiscriminate fury across the world less than two years
later, the World Health Organization admonished the world that it was "simply not ready" for the
pandemic.[92]

Advances in medical knowledge and technology, coupled with improved living standards and
public hygiene (at least in the developed world) have perhaps led to a certain complacency.
Vaccines and antibiotics made it possible to seemingly defeat invisible organisms, and yet, new
species of viruses and bacteria have appeared in recent history. HIV, SARS, Escherichia (*E.
coli*), dengue fever, Lyme disease and West Nile virus are all examples of persistent, previously
unknown morbidities that are rapidly increasing and spreading.[93]

The reasons for this are varied, involving changes in human demographics and environment,
economic and social conditions, as well as climate, wars, and famine. In the case of the
Coronavirus, it seems that the animal markets of Wuhan provided the ideal conditions for the
chance transmission of the virus from a bat to a human, which otherwise would have been
extremely unlikely.[94] That said, viruses fundamentally possess an extraordinary ability to adapt
and evolve. They are incredibly ancient, and studies suggest that viruses were infecting single-
celled organisms in the planet's primordial soup billions of years ago.[95] Viruses are not, strictly
speaking, alive, but they are composed of DNA or RNA[96] and have a high mutation rate, which
allows them to adapt to their hosts and evolve at a much faster rate than other protein-based

---

time in Geneva" https://www.who.int/news-room/detail/10-09-2018-global-preparedness-monitoring-board-
convenes-for-the-first-time-in-geneva.

[91] Ibid.

[92] Kate Lyons and Sarah Boseley, "Coronavirus spreads further as WHO expert warns world 'not ready' for
pandemic" *The Guardian* February 26, 2020 https://www.theguardian.com/world/2020/feb/26/coronavirus-spreads-
further-as-who-expert-warns-world-not-ready-for-pandemic.

[93] "Emerging infectious diseases", *John Hopkins Medicine* https://www.hopkinsmedicine.org/health/conditions-and-
diseases/emerging-infectious-diseases.

[94] "Birds, pigs and pangolins: why do viruses keep appearing in China?" *News.com.au*
https://www.news.com.au/world/bats-pigs-and-pangolins-why-do-viruses-keep-appearing-in-

china/video/23d22e2e71a8aea5977524da41b4cc7e.

[95] Mahy, W.J.; Van Regenmortel, MHV, eds. (2009). *Desk Encyclopedia of General Virology*. Academic Press, p.
25.
[96] Koonin EV, Senkevich TG, Dolja VV (September 2006). "The ancient Virus World and evolution of
cells". *Biology Direct*. **1** (1): 29.

organisms. This is why new strains of viruses appear and why some can become resistant to drugs.[97]

Ancient and medieval people obviously struggled in different ways to deal with pandemics, but to be fair, it does not seem as though humanity will be completely rid of the scourge of pestilence and the primordial terror of an unseen enemy that might end the human world anytime soon. Societies have moved into a scientific age that eschews the need for gods and priest-healers from the past, and they can dismiss notions of humors and miasma, but viruses and bacteria are still out there.

Online Resources

Other books about the plague on Amazon

Further Reading

Contributors, Harvard University Library. "The Great Plague of London, 1665." *Harvard University Library*. The President and Fellows of Harvard College, 2008. Web. 27 Mar. 2017. <http://ocp.hul.harvard.edu/contagion/plague.html>.

Ross, David. "The London Plague of 1665." *The London Plague of 1665*. David Ross, 2010. Web. 27 Mar. 2017. <http://www.britainexpress.com/History/plague.htm>.

Editors, UK National Archives. "Great Plague of 1665-1666." *The National Archives*. The National Archives Kew, Richmond, Surrey, 2015. Web. 27 Mar. 2017. <http://www.nationalarchives.gov.uk/education/resources/great-plague/>.

Stanbridge, Nicola. "DNA confirms cause of 1665 London's Great Plague." *BBC News*. BBC, 8 Sept. 2016. Web. 27 Mar. 2017. <http://www.bbc.com/news/science-environment-37287715>.

Fenn, Chris, Katy Stoddard, Apple Chan-Fardel, and Paul Torpey. "Mapping London's great plague of 1665." *The Guardian*. Guardian News and Media, Ltd., 12 Aug. 2015. Web. 27 Mar. 2017. <https://www.theguardian.com/society/ng-interactive/2015/aug/12/london-great-plague-1665-bills-of-mortality>.

Editors, BBC. "The Great Plague." *BBC Bitesize*. BBC, 2016. Web. 27 Mar. 2017. <http://www.bbc.co.uk/education/guides/zd3wxnb/revision/2>.

Authors, Snopes. "Ring Around the Rosie." *Snopes*. Proper Media, 12 July 2015. Web. 27 Mar. 2017. <http://www.snopes.com/language/literary/rosie.asp>.

---

[97] Boutwell CL, Rolland MM, Herbeck JT, Mullins JI, Allen TM (October 2010). "Viral evolution and escape during acute HIV-1 infection". *The Journal of Infectious Diseases*. **202** (Suppl 2): S309–14.

Smallwood, Karl. "TOADS AROUND YOUR NECK AND FORCING KIDS TO SMOKE-ESCAPING THE GREAT PLAGUE OF LONDON (1665-1666)." *Today I Found Out*. Today I Found Out, 27 May 2015. Web. 27 Mar. 2017. <http://www.todayifoundout.com/index.php/2015/05/great-plague-london/>.

Authors, The Black Death. "How does the nursery rhyme "Ring around the Rosie" Relate to the Black Death?" *The Black Death*. Blogspot, 17 May 2011. Web. 27 Mar. 2017. <http://theblackdeathkc.blogspot.tw/2011/05/how-does-nursery-rhyme-ring-around.html>.

Schladweiler, Jon. "The history of a nursery rhyme — Ring around the Rosie." *The History of Sanitary Sewers*. WordPress, 19 Feb. 2002. Web. 27 Mar. 2017. <http://www.sewerhistory.org/miscellaneous/the-history-of-a-nursery-rhyme-ring-around-the-rosie/>.

Benedictow, Ole J. "The Black Death: The Greatest Catastrophe Ever." *History Today*. History Today, Ltd., 3 Mar. 2005. Web. 27 Mar. 2017. <http://www.historytoday.com/ole-j-benedictow/black-death-greatest-catastrophe-ever>.

Stöppler, Melissa Conrad, MD. "Plague (Black Death)." *MedicineNet*. Ed. Steven Doerr. MedicineNet, Inc., 8 Oct. 2015. Web. 27 Mar. 2017. <http://www.medicinenet.com/plague_facts/article.htm>.

Editors, Healthline. "The Plague." *Healthline*. Healthline Media, 2016. Web. 27 Mar. 2017. <http://www.healthline.com/health/plague#Overview1>.

Authors, History Channel. "BLACK DEATH." *History Channel*. A&E Television Networks, LLC, 2015. Web. 27 Mar. 2017. <http://www.history.com/topics/black-death>.

Snell, Melissa. "The Spread of the Black Death through Europe." *Thought Company*. About, Inc., 13 Jan. 2017. Web. 27 Mar. 2017. <https://www.thoughtco.com/spread-of-the-black-death-through-europe-4123214>.

Hope, Jessica. "10 things you (probably) didn't know about the Black Death." *History Extra*. Immediate Media Company, 2 Nov. 2015. Web. 27 Mar. 2017. <http://www.historyextra.com/article/international-history/10-things-you-probably-didnt-know-about-black-death>.

Newman, Simon. "The Black Death." *The Finer Times*. The Finer Times, 8 Oct. 2014. Web. 28 Mar. 2017. <http://www.thefinertimes.com/Middle-Ages/the-black-death.html>.

Wheelis, Mark. "Biological Warfare at the 1346 Siege of Caffa." *Centers for Disease Control and Prevention*. CDC Media, 16 July 2010. Web. 28 Mar. 2017. <https://wwwnc.cdc.gov/eid/article/8/9/01-0536_article>.

Steve, Rick. "The Plague That Shook Medieval Europe." *Rick Steve's Europe*. Rick Steves' Europe, Inc., 2017. Web. 28 Mar. 2017. <https://www.ricksteves.com/watch-read-listen/read/articles/the-plague-that-shook-medieval-europe>.

Editors, SHSU. "Boccaccio describes the Plague in Florence in the Introduction of the Decameron." *Sam Houston State University*. Sam Houston State University, 2003. Web. 28 Mar. 2017. <http://www.shsu.edu/~his_ncp/Boccaccio.html>.

Pearce, Ian. "Black Death." *Great Ayton*. Great Ayton, May 2009. Web. 28 Mar. 2017. <http://greatayton.wdfiles.com/local--files/public-health/Black-Death.pdf>.

Editors, AF. "The plague in Milan." *Archivum Fabricae*. Veneranda Fabbrica del Duomo di Milano, Feb. 2015. Web. 28 Mar. 2017. <http://archivio.duomomilano.it/en/infopage/the-plague-in-milan/bfa2bcc5-5bbc-4729-9181-46f6646bece7/>.

Authors, Museum of London. "London Plagues 1348-1665." *Museum of London*. Museum of London, 2013. Web. 28 Mar. 2017. <https://www.museumoflondon.org.uk/application/files/5014/5434/6066/london-plagues-1348-1665.pdf>.

Williams, Chris. "ANATOMY OF A FLEA BITE." *Colonial Pest Control*. Colonial Pest Control, Inc., 11 Sept. 2014. Web. 28 Mar. 2017. <http://www.colonialpest.com/anatomy-of-a-flea-bite/>.

Authors, Sunday Times. "The novice's study." *Sunday Times*. Wijeya Newspapers, Ltd., 2006. Web. 28 Mar. 2017. <http://www.sundaytimes.lk/060702/plus/PlusP4.1.html>.

Editors, Stone Age Refugee. "How many valiant men..." *Stone Age Refugee*. WordPress, 24 Mar. 2011. Web. 28 Mar. 2017. <https://stoneagerefugee.wordpress.com/2011/03/24/how-many-valiant-men-how-many-fair-ladies-breakfast-with-their-kinfolk-and-the-same-night-supped-with-their-ancestors-in-the-next-world-the-condition-of-the-people-was-pitiable-to-behold-they-sick/>.

Frith, John. "The History of Plague – Part 1. The Three Great Pandemics." *Journal of Military and Veterans' Health*. Australasian Military Medicine Association, 4 Feb. 2012. Web. 28 Mar. 2017. <http://jmvh.org/article/the-history-of-plague-part-1-the-three-great-pandemics/>.

DNews. "Bubonic Plague Originated in China." *Seeker*. Group Nine Media, 1 Nov. 2010. Web. 28 Mar. 2017. <https://www.seeker.com/bubonic-plague-originated-in-china-1765135886.html>.

Walker, Cameron. "Bubonic Plague Traced to Ancient Egypt." *National Geographic News*.

National Geographic Society, 10 Mar. 2004. Web. 28 Mar. 2017.
<http://news.nationalgeographic.com/news/2004/03/0310_040310_blackdeath.html>.

Authors, Telegraph. "Medieval London: 10 disgusting facts." *The Telegraph*. Telegraph Media Group, Ltd., 5 Apr. 2011. Web. 29 Mar. 2017.
<http://www.telegraph.co.uk/culture/tvandradio/8421415/Medieval-London-10-disgusting-facts.html>.

Kollenborn, K. P. "15 Medieval Hygiene Practices That Might Make You Queasy." *K.P.Kollenborn*. Blogspot, 9 Jan. 2015. Web. 29 Mar. 2017.
<http://kpkollenborn.blogspot.tw/2014/11/15-medieval-hygiene-practices-that.html>.

Richter, Ash M. "13 Gross Medieval Hygiene Practices That Will Give You Nightmares." *All Day*. All Day, 2015. Web. 29 Mar. 2017. <http://www.allday.com/13-gross-medieval-hygiene-practices-that-will-give-you-nightmares-2180807051.html>.

Authors, GSSG. "Life in a Medieval Town." *Go Social Studies Go*. Wix, 2008. Web. 29 Mar. 2017. <http://www.gohistorygo.com/medieval-towns->.

Brown, Stephanie. "What did medieval people think caused the Black Death, and how did they respond accordingly?" *Gorffennol Student Journal*. British Conference of Undergraduate Research, Winter 2007. Web. 29 Mar. 2017. <http://gorffennol.swansea.ac.uk/wp-content/uploads/2016/01/2-Black-Death.pdf>.

Banks-Smith, Nancy. "Dead reckoning ." *The Guardian*. Guardian News and Media, Ltd., 16 Oct. 2001. Web. 29 Mar. 2017.
<https://www.theguardian.com/media/2001/oct/16/tvandradio.television1>.

Conlon, Katherine. "The Plague Pits of London." *Travel Darkly*. Travel Darkly, Ltd., 23 Apr. 2014. Web. 29 Mar. 2017. <http://www.traveldarkly.com/plague-pits-london/>.

Editors, Encyclopedia.Com. "Bills Of Mortality." *Encyclopedia.Com*. The Gale Group, Inc., 2002. Web. 30 Mar. 2017. <http://www.encyclopedia.com/history/modern-europe/british-and-irish-history/bills-mortality>.

Johnson, Ben. "The Great Plague." *Historic UK*. Historic UK, Ltd., 4 Jan. 2013. Web. 30 Mar. 2017. <http://www.historic-uk.com/HistoryUK/HistoryofEngland/The-Great-Plague/>.

Mason, Emma. "London's 7 most memorable lord mayors." *History Extra*. Immediate Media Company, 5 Sept. 2016. Web. 30 Mar. 2017.
<http://www.historyextra.com/article/feature/london-lord-mayors-history-7-most-memorable>.

Trueman, C. N. "The Lord Mayor's Orders." *The History Learning Site*. The History

Learning Site, Ltd., 17 Mar. 2015. Web. 30 Mar. 2017.
<http://www.historylearningsite.co.uk/stuart-england/the-lord-mayors-orders/>.

Trueman, C. N. "Eyam and the Great Plague of 1665." *The History Learning Site*. The History Learning Site, Ltd., 16 Aug. 2016. Web. 30 Mar. 2017.
<http://www.historylearningsite.co.uk/stuart-england/eyam-and-the-great-plague-of-1665/>.

Staff, Mayo Clinic. "Symptoms and causes." *Mayo Clinic*. Mayo Foundation for Medical Education and Research, 15 Mar. 2016. Web. 30 Mar. 2017.
<http://www.mayoclinic.org/diseases-conditions/plague/symptoms-causes/dxc-20196766>.

White, Frances. "Why did doctors during the Black Death wear 'beak masks'?" *History Answers*. Imagine Publishing Media, 2 June 2014. Web. 30 Mar. 2017.
<https://www.historyanswers.co.uk/people-politics/why-did-doctors-during-the-black-death-wear-beak-masks/>.

Birkwood, Katie. "For the cure of the plague." *Royal College of Physicians*. The Royal College of Physicians of London, 15 May 2015. Web. 30 Mar. 2017.
<https://www.rcplondon.ac.uk/news/cure-plague>.

Editors, RCP. "Plague remedies from the garden." *Royal College of Physicians*. The Royal College of Physicians of London, 4 Aug. 2015. Web. 30 Mar. 2017.
<https://www.rcplondon.ac.uk/news/plague-remedies-garden>.

Smith, Lisa. "Tag: Pest House Fields." *The Sloane Letters Project*. University of Saskatchewan , 15 Mar. 2013. Web. 30 Mar. 2017. <http://sloaneletters.com/tag/pest-house-fields/>.

Shariff, Mohammed. "10 Crazy Cures for the Black Death." *Listverse*. Listverse, Ltd., 21 Jan. 2013. Web. 31 Mar. 2017. <http://listverse.com/2013/01/21/10-crazy-cures-for-the-black-death/>.

Johnson, Ben. "The Great Fire of London." *Historic UK*. Historic UK, Ltd., 3 Sept. 2016. Web. 31 Mar. 2017. <http://www.historic-uk.com/HistoryUK/HistoryofEngland/The-Great-Fire-of-London/>.

Authors, The Week. "What was Black Death and how did it end?" *The Week*. The Week, Ltd., 31 Aug. 2016. Web. 31 Mar. 2017. <http://www.theweek.co.uk/76088/what-was-black-death-and-how-did-it-end>.

Morelle, Rebecca. "'Gerbils replace rats' as main cause of Black Death." *BBC News*. BBC, 24 Feb. 2015. Web. 31 Mar. 2017. <http://www.bbc.com/news/science-environment-31588671>.

Editors, Wikipedia. "Theories of the Black Death." *Wikpedia.* Wikimedia Foundation, Inc., 1 Mar. 2017. Web. 31 Mar. 2017. <https://en.wikipedia.org/wiki/Theories_of_the_Black_Death#Ebola-like_virus>.

Creighton, Charles. *A History of Epidemics in Britain: From AD 664 to the Extinction of Plague.* Vol. 1. N.p.: Cambridge U Press, 2013. Print.

Hughes, Robert. *Barcelona.* N.p.: Vintage, 1993. Print.

Gill, John. *Andalucia: A Cultural History (Landscapes of the Imagination).* N.p.: Oxford U Press, 2008. Print.

Porter, Stephen. *The Great Plague.* N.p.: Sutton Pub Ltd, 2000. Print.

Hays, Jo N. *Epidemics and Pandemics: Their Impacts on Human History.* 1st ed. N.p.: ABC-CLIO, 2005. Print.

Stone, Jon R. *The Routledge Dictionary of Latin Quotations: The Illiterati's Guide to Latin Maxims, Mottoes, Proverbs, and Sayings (Latin for the Illiterati).* Bilingual ed. N.p.: Routledge, 2004. Print.

Gaskill, Malcolm. *Witchfinders: A Seventeenth-Century English Tragedy.* N.p.: Harvard U Press, 2007. Print.

Jones, Becky, and Clare Lewis. *The Bumper Book of London: Everything You Need to Know About London and More... .* N.p.: Frances Lincoln, 2012. Print.

Moote, A. Lloyd, and Dorothy C. Moote. *The Great Plague: The Story of London's Most Deadly Year .* 1st ed. N.p.: Johns Hopkins U Press, 2006. Print.

Wright, Cindy. *The Dark Traveller.* N.p.: Lulu.Com, 2012. Print.

Withington, John. *London's Disasters: From Boudicca to the Banking Crisis.* N.p.: The History Press, 2010. Print.

Hayden, Deborah. *Pox: Genius, Madness, And The Mysteries Of Syphilis.* Reprint ed. N.p.: Basic , 2003. Print.

Hyde, Edward. *The History of the Rebellion and Civil Wars in England Begun in the Year 1641: (History of the Rebellion & Civil Wars in England Begun in the Year 1641) .* Ed. W. Dunn Macray. Vol. 5. N.p.: Clarendon Press, 1993. Print.

Appleby, Andrew B. *The Disappearance of Plague: A Continuing Puzzle.* N.p.: Economic History Society, 1980. Print.

N.p. "The Great Plague." *Plague, Fire, War and Treason: A Century of Troubles*. Channel 4. London, 31 Oct. 2005. Television.

Oliver, Dan. "Secrets of the Great Plague ." *Secrets of the Great Plague*. Dir. Tom Pollock. Atlantic Productions See. 28 Aug. 2006. Television.

Free Books by Charles River Editors

We have brand new titles available for free most days of the week. To see which of our titles are currently free, click on this link.

Discounted Books by Charles River Editors

We have titles at a discount price of just 99 cents everyday. To see which of our titles are currently 99 cents, click on this link.